Twayne's English Authors Series

Sylvia E. Bowman, *Editor*

INDIANA UNIVERSITY

Katherine Mansfield

(TEAS) 23

Katherine Mansfield

By SARALYN R. DALY

Twayne Publishers, Inc.   ::   New York

To Jan and Bruce

who, more or less, lived with **it**

Preface

The formulative influence of Katherine Mansfield on the development of modern fiction is remarked in any literary history and acknowledged in most anthologies of the modern short story. Though dead for forty years, her reputation is international. Perhaps because so many of her personal papers—letters, notebooks, drafts of unfinished stories—have been published, comprehensive critical studies have dwelt on the interrelations of her life and works. The most valuable of these was by Sylvia Berkman and appeared in 1951. It was followed in 1954 by Antony Alpers' definitive biography, which also undertook some critical considerations. Since these publications, attention has focused largely on explications of a few of the major stories.

Literary fashions change not quite so rapidly as graduate schools feel compelled to develop new seminars or "little magazines" arise and vanish. So it has been with Katherine Mansfield; a period of maudlin adulation attendant upon her early death led finally to serious consideration of her work. Then, as the content of fiction shifted to more obviously "social" themes, articulated philosophies, and hard-boiled objectivity, there developed a tendency to admire, sometimes perfunctorily, her craftsmanship but to underrate her subject matter and to overlook her depth. Thus it is time again to appraise the writing of Miss Mansfield, to examine her developing technique and its influence, to seek, perhaps more rigorously, the meaning of her stories. These are the purposes of this critical study of her fiction. Her poetry and book reviews are negligible and will not be considered. Her letters, *Scrapbook*, and *Journal* are mentioned only when they shed light on the fiction.

Katherine Mansfield attempts to view the progress in form and meaning of Miss Mansfield's work. The first chapter reviews her literary career and the direction given it by the events of her life. Chapters 2 and 3 analyze her early work and the influence upon it of Anton Chekhov's writing, periodical publication, and the milieu in which she wrote. Her turning point in craft and her crystalization of attitude, manifest in "Prelude" and "Je ne Parle pas Français," are the subject of Chapter 4. In Chapter 5 Miss Mansfield's typical subjects and lines of thought are examined. Chapter 6 appraises the final form and view of the artist, the variety of her writing, and her place in the literary context.

It is hoped that this detailed examination of many of the short stories will recall to readers of Katherine Mansfield the vitality, depth, and contemporary relevance of her work.

SARALYN R. DALY

La Canada, California

Acknowledgments

I am indebted to the following for permission to reprint material in this book:

Constable and Company, Limited, for permission to quote from *The Aloe* and *Journal of Katherine Mansfield*, by Katherine Mansfield.

Critique, for permission to quote from "Katherine Mansfield: Plagiarist, Disciple, or Ardent Admirer?" by Ronald Sutherland.

Harcourt, Brace and World, Inc., for permission to quote from *A Writer's Diary* by Virginia Woolf.

The Hogarth Press and Mr. Leonard Woolf, for permission to quote from *A Haunted House* and *The Waves* by Virginia Woolf.

Alfred A. Knopf, Inc., for permission to quote from *The Letters of Katherine Mansfield, Katherine Mansfield's Letters to John Middleton Murry, 1913-1922, The Scrapbook*, and *The Short Stories of Katherine Mansfield*, by Katherine Mansfield.

It is a pleasure, moreover, to thank the librarians of the Hoover Institute, Palo Alto, California, and of the Huntington Library, San Marino, California, for their generous assistance and unfailing hospitality.

I am also grateful to the Los Angeles State College Foundation for a study-grant which helped support some of my research.

Contents

Chronology

1888   Katherine Mansfield born, October 14, in Wellington, New Zealand, daughter of Harold Beauchamp and Annie Burnell (Dyer) Beauchamp.

1895-   Attended Karori State School, Wellington, New Zealand.
1898

1898-   Attended Wellington Girls' High School, Wellington, New
1899   Zealand. Published twice in the *High School Reporter*.

1900   Attended Miss Swainson's private school, Wellington, New Zealand. Founded a magazine, *The School*, handwritten.

1903-   Attended Queen's College, London. Five sketches pub-
1906   lished in *Queen's College Magazine*. Returned to New Zealand.

1907   Three sketches and a poem published in the Melbourne *Native Companion*.

1908   "Study: The Death of a Rose" published in *Triad*. Returned to London.

1909   March 2, married George Bowden; left him the next day. Member of the chorus of a traveling light-opera company. Pregnant, lodged by her mother in a convent, Bavaria. Lodged with postmistress, Wörishofen, Bavaria. Had a miscarriage.

1910   Returned to London; lived briefly with her husband. February, March, May, July, August, publication in the *New Age*. Abdominal operation; rheumatic fever.

1911   Spring, had an abortion. May, June, August, September, October, publication in the *New Age*. July, pleurisy in Bruges, Belgium, and Geneva, Switzerland. September, returned to London. December, *In a German Pension* published.

1912   Met John Middleton Murry. March, publication in the

New Age. Spring, "The Woman at the Store" published in *Rhythm.* April, John Middleton Murry moved into Miss Mansfield's flat. May, in Paris with Murry. Fall, Stephen Swift, publisher, vanished, leaving *Rhythm* debts.

1912-
1913   Co-editor of *Rhythm,* June to March. Many publications.

1913   March, last issue of *Rhythm.* May-July, four stories published in the *Blue Review,* which then failed. Worked as a film extra. December, in Paris, wrote "Something Childish But Very Natural."

1914   February, returned to London. October, lived near D. H. and Frieda Lawrence, near Cholesbury.

1915   February, her brother Leslie Beauchamp in London to join his regiment. Three trips to Paris, stayed in Francis Carco's flat. October 7, Leslie Beauchamp killed at Ploegsteert Wood. October and November, three stories published in four issues of the *Signature,* which then failed. November, began residence in Bandol, France. November 4, "Stay-Laces" published in the *New Age.*

1916   April, lived in North Cornwall near Lawrence. May, moved to South Cornwall. Fall, returned to London.

1917   May, June, September, October, publication in the *New Age.* "The Aloe" rewritten as *Prelude.*

1918   January, resumed residence in Bandol. February 19, had first hemorrhage. Wrote "Je ne Parle pas Français." March in Paris, caught in the "Big Bertha" bombardment. April, returned to London. April 29, divorced by George Bowden. May 3, married John Middleton Murry. June, *Prelude* published by the Hogarth Press. August 8, death of her mother. "Bliss" published in the *English Review.* Winter, Murry became editor of the *Athenaeum.* Began book reviews for the *Athenaeum.*

1919   April-August, poetry published in the *Athenaeum* under pseudonym, "Elizabeth Stanley." April-October, Chekhov letters translated with Koteliansky published in the *Athenaeum.* September, began residence in Ospedaletti, Italy. December, sent "The New Husband" verses to Murry.

1920   January 11, wrote "The Man Without a Temperament." January, moved to Menton, France. April, returned to

London. June-December, publication of stories in the *Athenaeum*. December, *Bliss and Other Stories* published by Constable. September, returned to Menton, France. October-December, wrote "The Life of Ma Parker," "Miss Brill," "The Young Girl," "The Stranger," "Poison," "The Daughters of the Late Colonel," and other stories.

1921 February 26, "The Life of Ma Parker" published in the *Nation*. May, began residence in Switzerland. July, living at Montana, Switzerland. July-January, wrote "At the Bay," "The Garden-Party," "The Doll's House," "A Cup of Tea," "Marriage à la Mode," "Her First Ball," "An Ideal Family," "Mr. and Mrs. Dove," "The Voyage," and other stories.

1922 January, "At the Bay" published in the *London Mercury*. February, "The Garden-Party" serialized in the *Westminster Weekly Gazette;* in Paris for radium treatment for tuberculosis; "The Doll's House" published in the *Nation;* wrote "The Fly"; *The Garden-Party and Other Stories* published by Constable. March 18, "The Fly" published in the *Nation*. April 29, "Honeymoon" published in the *Nation*. May, finished first course of radium treatments. June, returned to Sierre, Switzerland. July, wrote "The Canary." August 14, made her will, naming Murry literary executor. August, returned to London. August-September, translated, with Koteliansky, Gorki's *Reminiscences of Leonid Andreyev*. September, underwent second course of radium treatments. October 17, entered the Gurdjieff Institute, Fontainebleau, France.

1923 January 9, died of a hemorrhage. Buried January 12 in the Protestant cemetery, Avon, Fontainebleau, France.

CHAPTER 1

"Out of This Nettle, Danger"

I

THE observable elements which molded Katherine Mansfield (née Kathleen Mansfield Beauchamp) are those which seem to have shaped many artists—conflicts with environment, rootlessness, a permanent sense of alienation. Less than three years before her death she composed an oddly revealing "Biographical Note":

> Née 14 Octobre à Nouvelle Zelande
> Premier voyage âge de six mois
> Premier histoire publiée âge de neuf ans
> Le reste de ma vie est passé en voyageant et en écrivant des "short stories". . . .
> Wife of the brilliant poète et critique J. M. M. who is the famous editor of the newly brought to life and prominent Athenaeum.
> Two cats.[1]
>
> K. M.[2]

The brief mention of the cats laconically minimizes the excessive, perhaps teasing, flattery of John Middleton Murry. But the rhythms of repeated structures and echoing words, even in this whimsical record, are those of the practiced writer who reveals her own image. "Premier voyage . . . Premier histoire . . . ," she writes and then, "Le reste de ma vie . . . voyageant . . . écrivant. . . ." First trip . . . first story . . . wandering and writing. Thus she had spent her life. These were the things she had done and, like it or not, these were the things that had mattered. So, toward the end, Miss Mansfield set down her homelessness as though, from the beginning, it had been interwoven with her writing.

Certainly for a long time she remembered her youth as difficult.

The New Zealand stories and some of those in *In a German Pension* reflect Miss Mansfield's gradually maturing appraisal of her childhood. The early stories are personal accounts of a child neglected by all but the grandmother, ignored or criticized by the mother, frightened and unjustly punished by the self-centered, authoritarian father. Later the more objective artist portrays an adventurous, imaginative, self-sustaining Kezia, still essentially alone amid many children and older relations. Chronically invalid and aloof, the mother rejects the entire family. The father is bluff, hearty, perhaps insensitive to others, but pathetically vulnerable. As early as 1915 Miss Mansfield could write of her father, "He was young and sensitive still. He still wondered whether in the deepest sense he got his money's worth." [3]

The accounts of others [4] confirm her own impressions of a child at cross-purposes with her elders. Though Kathleen Beauchamp wrote for school publications throughout her girlhood, she was remembered for something else. She had founded a magazine at Miss Swainson's private school in Wellington, but the teachers recalled her compositions only as "poorly written, poorly spelled, and careless"; her behavior as "not even cleverly naughty." [5] She was the unpromising, rebellious girl who might call her father "Bottlenose"; despite prohibitions, she would probably show the new doll's house to the washerwoman's bedraggled children.

Sent to London in her fifteenth year for further education, Kathleen Beauchamp glimpsed another world. She claimed later to have learned little in her three years at Queen's College, but dreamily and romantically she absorbed the atmosphere: "My college life . . . might never have contained a book or a lecture. I lived in the girls, the professor, the big lovely building, the leaping fires in winter and the abundant flowers in summer. The views out the windows, all the pattern that was—weaving. Nobody saw it, I felt, as I did." [6]

When three years later she returned reluctantly to New Zealand, she was collecting and herself composing Wildean epigrams. A selection reflects her struggle with the family, her determination to develop as an artist, and her naïve conviction that the way lay through the cultivation of what the Decadents had called "experience." Earnestly she copied the advice of her masters or composed on their models:

"Out of This Nettle, Danger"

"To be premature is to be perfect."—O. W. [Oscar Wilde]

"To acknowledge the presence of fear is to give birth to failure."—K. M. [She had chosen her penname by this time.]

"The strongest man is he who stands most alone."—Henrik Ibsen.

"Push everything as far as it will go."—O. W.

"No life is spoiled but one whose growth is arrested."—O. W.

"If you want to mar a nature, you have merely to reform it."—O. W.

"The only way to get rid of temptation is to yield to it."—O. W.

"To realize one's nature perfectly—that is what each of us is here for."—O. W.[7]

Somehow, after a year and a half of conflict, she won an annual allowance of one hundred pounds from her father and on July 9, 1908, sailed for England.

Determined on self-realization, she began an erratic, undisciplined life. On March 2, 1909, she married George Bowden. a musician eleven years her senior; on the following day she left him. In May she was pregnant by another man, and before the year ended she had a miscarriage. However, this mischance, in that it sent her to Bavaria, was of literary benefit. For there she read for the first time short stories by Anton Chekhov,[8] whose work confirmed her developing artistic instincts. And in Bavaria she made the observations which became the stories of *In a German Pension*.

Back in London in 1910, Katherine Mansfield began what seemed to be a successful literary life. Her sardonic, immature stories appeared regularly in the *New Age*, a socialist publication intent on challenging a world still reminiscent of Queen Victoria. Later a meeting with John Middleton Murry drew her even more into an artistic milieu. She experimented in various story forms, too often writing to suit the editorial policies of the magazines—*Rhythm*, the *Blue Review*, and *Signature*—she and Murry edited between 1912 and 1915.

During these years her uneasy alliance with Murry became permanent. Their life together, however, never left Miss Mansfield with the feeling that she at last had roots. Instead, the interruptions of their relationship by her need to travel for the sake of health probably intensified her loneliness. Gradually she discovered, too, that amid London's Bohemia and in much of Murry's world she remained alien. Entries in her journal of spring, 1914, are characteristic: "And I am sure J. [Murry] could get a great deal of pleasure out of pleasant society. I couldn't. I've done with it, and can't contact it at all now. I had so much rather lean idly over the bridge and watch the boats and the free, unfamiliar people and feel the wind blow. No, I hate society." [9] A few days later she wrote: "I feel a real horror of people closing over me. I could not *bear* them." [10]

After the *Blue Review* failed in 1913, she and Murry spent the winter in Paris. There, untied to any editorial policy, Miss Mansfield wrote her first long story, "Something Childish But Very Natural." Still between magazines in the spring of 1915, she made an illegal visit to the French front to visit the young writer Francis Carco. The result was another long story, "An Indiscreet Journey." Neither of these works seems designed for any audience then available to Miss Mansfield. Neither was published in her lifetime, but both marked a distinct technical and emotional change in her writing, and "An Indiscreet Journey" evidenced her developing social consciousness under the impact of World War I. Shortly after the completion of the latter story she began "The Aloe," intended to be a novel about her New Zealand life.

In the looser form of these stories, Katherine Mansfield let extended detail reveal by implication meanings more sympathetic than she usually attempted. After the death of her brother Leslie in October, 1915, she asserted in her journal, "I feel I have a duty to perform to the lovely time when we were both alive. I want to write about it." [11] But her work did not continue in that vein. She struggled with "The Aloe" during 1916 but could not turn it into the sensitive and perceptive "Prelude" until the summer of the following year. Meanwhile she returned to her terse, sardonic *New Age* manner. One story appeared in that publication in 1915 and ten between May and October of 1917. And the deeply caustic "Je ne Parle pas Français," written in February, 1918, she excitedly described as her technical turning point.[12] Clearly, in this indecisive period, she was artistically homeless as well as emotionally bereft.

Before the war ended, the pattern of her life was established. Every winter since 1914 she had suffered illness of some sort and there had been a sojourn in France, sometimes on the doctor's advice. On February 19, 1918, she had her first tubercular hemor-

,hage. Fortunately Ida Baker, the faithful friend from Queen's College days, was on hand to care for her. Together in March and April they suffered the "Big Bertha" bombardment of Paris. Then, freed after nine years by the divorce Bowden had secured, Miss Mansfield was able to marry Murry on May 3, but within two weeks she.had to leave him for the sake of her health. At the end of June they were together again, and so the pendulum continued to swing. Incessantly wandering in search of a healthy climate, lamenting her aloneness when she must part from her husband, Katherine Mansfield disciplined herself to see more clearly, to write better, "truer" stories.

Her literary career became solidly established. *Prelude* was published in 1918 as a small book by the Hogarth Press, and Miss Mansfield began an uncomfortable acquaintance with Virginia Woolf. The *English Review* published "Bliss" in June. When, that winter, Murry became the editor of the *Athenaeum*, his wife became a regular book reviewer. She also contributed, with S. S. Koteliansky, translations of some Chekhov letters. In June, 1920, the *Athenaeum* began to publish stories: Miss Mansfield supplied eight by December and wrote three others for other magazines. *Bliss and Other Stories*, published in December of that year, received favorable critical comment. Though Miss Mansfield was by no means satisfied with her work, she had arrived. Praise and criticism usually reached her by mail, for, with the increasing seriousness of her tuberculosis, she could rarely risk living in the English climate. In this state of physical remoteness, her fictional world became more vividly and more complexly realized.

Despite, perhaps because of, her illness, her story output grew almost feverish. Between November, 1920, and July, 1922, twenty-one months, she completed her work with at least twenty stories, a number of fragments, and the beginning of a novel. Many of these found instant periodical publication and were then collected in *The Garden-Party*, which appeared in February, 1922. There were two tremendous spurts: between October and December, 1920, Miss Mansfield wrote eight stories, among them six of her finest; again from July to December, 1921, while living with Murry in Switzerland, she wrote twelve stories, some merely to fulfill a contract with *Sphere;* but among them are five of her best. In February, 1922, she wrote "The Fly," and she was planning another volume while she underwent a new series of radium treatments in Paris. In July, back in Switzerland with Miss Baker while Murry lived nearby and visited her on weekends, she wrote "The Canary," her last completed story.

The next month Katherine Mansfield made her will, in which she instructed Murry to destroy her unfinished work and personal papers. That he did not is perhaps a service to the literary critic, but the fragmentary manner in which he released her "remains" probably served only to create a confused image of the developing artist. In London Miss Mansfield underwent a second course of radium treatments, but she had lost faith in their efficacy. Instead, she decided, she must cure herself by mystic means. With this in mind, she returned to France and in October entered the Gurdjieff Institute at Fontainebleau.

On January 9, 1923, Murry came for a belated holiday visit. Miss Mansfield was radiantly happy with him during the afternoon and evening. Then, as she started upstairs to bed, a violent hemorrhage began, and within a few minutes she was dead. The Shakespearean epigraph she used on the title page of *Bliss* serves for her tombstone inscription: "But I tell you, my lord fool, out of this nettle, danger, we pluck this flower, safety."

II

From the experience of her thirty-four years Katherine Mansfield shaped her stories. Her time and scope were limited. But— when with illness the scope decreased and the time, she knew, shortened—her production intensified and her utterance deepened. In 1908, as she began an independent life in London, her writing merely reflected her feeling of homelessness. In this she heads a long line of twentieth-century writers who cannot go home again, but whose imaginative will often returns. To her, as to many, adventures in Bohemia proved painful.

In self-defense the little colonial learned, but was not deceived by, the brittle mask of sophistication. The overdone satirical recoil characteristic of *In a German Pension* and of "Sunday Lunch" measures the extent of her pain. Apparently she never completely learned to protect herself. During tea one April afternoon in 1919, Virginia Woolf observed that she was "oddly hurt. . . . Her hard composure is much on the surface." [13] Yet Miss Mansfield had by that time completed in "Bliss" the exploratory appraisal of the world that revolves around the arts, and by the end of 1921 she would record her conclusions in "Marriage à la Mode."

She failed among the intelligentsia because she was interested in people and natural beauty, not in the painstaking analysis of ideas. In two years of steady work reviewing books for the *Athenaeum* she merely wasted herself and earned a little needed money: no critical theory appeared to concern her; she formulated none. D. H. Lawrence's 1914 escapist project of founding an ideal community on an island was discouraged by Katherine Mansfield of New Zealand, who confronted him with the statistics on actual island life. She would often record at great length the remarks of a humble maid or gardener, but the endless philosophical and spiritual conversations of Murry with J. D. Fergusson, Gordon Campbell, or Lawrence she found unprofitable. Practicality, openness, simplicity touched her heart, as did the beauty of flowers or the sea. A notable characteristic of her work was always immediacy of sense impressions and individualized response to them.

It was possibly a benefit that illness increasingly imposed upon her withdrawal from the literary society she disliked. But it also limited the data on which she based her final view of man's condition: isolated, with hope of neither human understanding nor supernatural help or pity. Though she gallantly affirmed beauty to the very end, the casual destructive forces always lurked nearby, and in any joy sadness waited. Katherine Mansfield's life taught her to admire the rose but, in her own repeated image, to look for "the snail under the leaf."

Perhaps she always instinctively knew and resisted this negation. "The Tiredness of Rosabel," written in 1908 when she began her London career, contains the seeds of many later stories and of the characteristic Mansfield technique. The story concerns the wish-fulfillment reverie of a girl whose "heritage was that tragic optimism, which is all too often the only inheritance of youth." From this shopgirl who returns to her drab room, hungry because she bought violets instead of dinner, arises a downward progress of impoverished women who awake, the dreaming over, to angry landladies and dreary choices. Viola of "The Swing of the Pendulum" flirts with a strange man but recoils at the realism of his intentions. In "Pictures" the older, defeated Ada Moss, wearing artificial violets, yields at last to prostitution to get the dinner Rosabel could go without. The tragic optimism has run out.

The technique of "The Tiredness of Rosabel" is similarly prophetic. It begins in the middle of the situation, which is delineated through the observations of Rosabel as she rides a bus home from work. Antithetic images lead to the antithetic conclusion. Dull, dirty streets are turned to opal and silver, even to Venice, in the view of the romantic girl. Human ambivalence appears as she thinks of herself in the very language she had scorned when scanning a cheap novel over another girl's shoulder on the bus. The insolent, suggestive Harry, though he insulted her in the shop, is desirable. Throughout the reverie, while Rosabel sees herself as exotically rich and then as romantically married to Harry, her fatigue recurs thematically. Nor is the odor of violets or her longing for dinner forgotten. The story remains within Rosabel's consciousness, flowing smoothly back in time, then forward in reverie, but maintaining awareness always of the present Rosabel, hungry and tired in her drab little room. Only after Rosabel has fallen asleep does the author intrude (unnecessarily, but Miss Mansfield has not yet learned this) for a compassionate summation. In shape and to some extent style, the story is like many Miss Mansfield will compose. Even her last completed story, "The Canary," takes place entirely in the consciousness of a woman who seems to speak first in the present, then of the past, and finally, to sum up, in the present again. Nor is there in that last story much alteration of the writer's attitude.

The technique of "The Tiredness of Rosabel" is not striking today, but for 1908 it is an astonishing departure. Miss Mansfield was not only emotionally and physically homeless at that time; she was artistically isolated. It is unlikely that she had yet read any Chekhov.[14] No departures from English storytelling traditions informed or supported her exploration of the craft. James Joyce had finished all but three stories of *Dubliners* in 1905, but he could not get the book published until 1914.[15] Virginia Woolf published no novels before 1915 and no stories before 1917, but, when her stories did appear, they were very much in the Mansfield manner, marked by the same personal immediacy of view, the same acute perception of detail. In the summer of 1917, after their first meeting, Miss Mansfield wrote Mrs. Woolf of the likeness: ". . . we have got the same job, Virginia, and it is really very curious and thrilling that we should both . . . be after so very nearly the same thing. We are, you know: there's no denying it." [16]

If in 1908 Katherine Mansfield had read Conrad, Stephen Crane, E. M. Forster, Bennett, or Galsworthy (to name a few contemporary writers of reputation), she found in them traditional form. The older style of story, from which Miss Mansfield departed immediately, relied heavily on a plot in which "something happened": a significant change in the situation, with stress on a climax and a conclusion. In "The Tiredness of Rosabel" there is no change and very little action. The author, despite her final intrusion, relies upon the reader to make the inferences necessary to understand the emotional suggestions of her story. It is a static episode, very free in its substitution of emotional for chronological order. Though not baldly so, the intended effect is painful, an effect of caustic pathos.[17] The reader is expected to recognize that, though there is sympathy for the sleeping Rosabel, there has been mockery implicit in the account of her daydream.

The story is distinctly modern, so far in advance of many of those to appear in *In a German Pension,* that one wonders whether the editorial policy of the *New Age,* Miss Mansfield's first London publisher, interfered in these stories with an artistic development which had to rely more heavily on the intelligence and sensitivity of the reader than editors striving for popular circulation are usually willing to do. For about five years the taste and probably the environments of the *New Age* and of *Rhythm* retarded Miss Mansfield's experimentation. Only toward the end of 1913, when she lacked a ready publisher, did she begin to find her way back to and to go beyond the achievement of "Rosabel."

CHAPTER 2

In a German Pension *and the* New Age

I

KATHERINE MANSFIELD'S first professional publication in England, "The Child-Who-Was-Tired," is so nearly like Chekhov's "Spat Khochetsia" that the question of plagiarism has often been argued.[1] The most reasonable view is that of Ronald Sutherland, who finds in the parallels between the two stories no plagiarism or imitation "save the commonplace appropriation of a thematic idea and plot detail from the storehouse of existing literature."[2] Sutherland, indeed, though he acknowledges probable borrowing of ideas in four instances—this one, "Marriage à la Mode," "Taking the Veil," and "The Fly"—concludes that in each case Miss Mansfield "produced a story characteristic of herself and entirely foreign to Anton Chekhov" and that he "in no significant way influenced" her writing.[3]

Certainly she found in Chekhov approaches congenial to her own developing literary impulse, and in borrowing his materials she altered them enough to make them her own. Though she would never "play the sedulous ape," the discovery of a kindred feeling and intention in short-story form was undoubtedly encouraging. In her highly individual way, and as inexplicably, her literary development parallels in broad outline Chekhov's move from immature caricatures and comic anecdotes written swiftly for daily and weekly papers to short stories which are the foundation of the contemporary tradition in fiction.

The German translation "Schlafen" is found in Volume IV of the Chekhov *Gesammelte Werke,* but perhaps more influential for the author of *In a German Pension* is Volume I, which contains "Humorische Geschichte."[4] Here Miss Mansfield would have found the "vaudeville element," which Renata Pogglioli calls "a lasting, or . . . recurring, ingredient in [Chekhov's] narrative work."[5] The *pension* stories are to a large extent results of Miss

In a German Pension *and the* New Age

Mansfield's Bavarian experience, but such pieces as "The Baron," "The Sister of the Baroness," "Frau Fischer," and "The Modern Soul" with their obvious yet dryly comic final illuminations take on the shape and tone of Chekhov's pre-1886 journalism. As with Chekhov, the introduction of compassion to the characterization of later stories adds a moral dimension which changes the humor to an irony not always amusing. Depth has increased immeasurably between the last sentence of "A Birthday" and the last sentence of "The Fly," but the anecdotal patterning defined by those final words is the same.

Katherine Mansfield is often credited with reinforcing Chekhov's influence on English writing. But it was an already created admiration of his manner which resulted in the acceptance of her work by the *New Age*. In 1909 Arnold Bennett, under the guise of "Jacob Tonson," had praised the Russian highly in that very periodical. His remarks were the culmination of a taste which had been developing since the first Chekhov translations had begun to appear in the 1890's. The translation of thirteen volumes of his short stories by Constance Garnett between 1916 and 1922 probably did more to influence the development of English fiction than the few slender Mansfield volumes.

Moreover, in 1910, when the *New Age* began enthusiastically to publish almost all the prose Miss Mansfield wrote for two years,[6] she pleased with more than her resemblance to Chekhov. Literary criticism was in the hands of A. E. Randall, who, Paul Selver remembers, specialized in "scathing wit" and based his "caustic effectiveness on a rather scanty stock of ideas." Trevor Allen favored the weekly with "sulphuric parodies," victimizing "the sillier poetasters of the time." T. E. Hulme provided, besides philosophy, anti-German bias.[7] The mood of the publication clearly welcomed, therefore, the sort of stories that made up Katherine Mansfield's first book, of which she wrote to John Middleton Murry ten years later: "I cannot have the *German Pension* republished under any circumstances. It is far too *immature* and I don't even acknowledge it today. I mean I don't 'hold' by it. I can't go foisting that kind of stuff on the public— *it's not good enough. . . .* It's positively juvenile, and besides it's not what I mean: it's a lie." [8]

What became a "lie" to the author of "Prelude" was probably

exactly what had won her acceptance in the *New Age:* the caustic lack of compassion and the emotional and intellectual limitations so frequently but undeliberately exposed in the complacent protagonist, clearly the persona of the Katherine Mansfield of 1910. The technical inadequacy must also have chagrined a writer as sternly critical of her work as the later Mansfield had become. Some of the sketches of Germans living *en pension* read like what they no doubt were: the slightly touched up journal of an embittered, defensive colonial girl who has mistaken her provincial literary success for sophistication.

The stories did not appear regularly in the *New Age.* There were four periods of literary output separated by periods of silence. These gaps indicate either that some of the stories were not written in Bavaria or that they demanded considerable rewriting after Miss Mansfield began to publish. Later she wrote gratefully to the editor, A. R. Orage, "you taught me how to write." [9] It may be possible to detect the nature of his instructions by examining her work in four segments.

Between February 24 and March 24, 1910, appeared "The Child-Who-Was-Tired," "Germans at Meat," "The Baron," and "The Luft Bad." In the July and August issues there were four more: "At Lehmann's," "Frau Brechenmacher Attends a Wedding," "The Sister of the Baroness," and "Frau Fischer." After an eight-month absence, consistent publication resumed in May, 1911. By September five stories and an uncollected sketch were printed. The stories were "A Birthday," "The Modern Soul," "The Breidenbach Family in England," "The Journey to Bruges," and "Being a Truthful Adventure." The last three, dated 1910 by Murry,[10] were not collected in *In a German Pension.* However, the volume did include "The Swing of the Pendulum," "A Blaze," and "The Advanced Lady," none of which had been published before.

II

Of the first group, "The Child-Who-Was-Tired" stands apart, having no connection with the *pension* scene of the other stories. The longing of the child for annihilation is thematically suggested by her repeated dozing into or attempting to tell the dream of "a little white road that led to nowhere, and where nobody walked at all." The story begins in this dream and moves through a day of longing for the "little white road"; then, as the observations of the child grow more and more fatigued and hallucinatory—people are alternately giants and dolls—and the conversation of the adults indicates that she is a half-wit, the child has her "beautiful marvellous idea." Laughing and clapping her hands, she suffocates the baby and at last escapes into her dream. The lack of reality in the major part of the child's day and expectations is enhanced by the abstract designations of the main characters: the Man, the Frau, the Child-Who-Was-Tired. In contrast to these are the children with real names—Anton, Hans, and Lena—who quarrel viciously and are dressed, fed, and beaten before disappearing to school.[11] The tasks of the day—the potatoes, the laundry, the baby—which burden the child, the grass in the meadow, the people on the real road down which she longs to escape to the dreamed of road, all are solidly perceived. Thus a rhythm of alternately focused reality and unfocused hallucination is achieved.

The narrative is flawed only by a few failures in diction, which break momentarily the illusion of the child's viewpoint. She looks at her arms "as if to scold them for being so thin, so much like little stunted twigs." She sees the sleeping children lying "in attitudes of mutual amity which certainly never existed out of their sleeping hours." The passage which follows is frequently out of control. But the lapse is brief, and aside from that this is a very well built story and conveys a strong impression.

The tone of the three German pieces (despite "the Frau," "The Child-Who-Was-Tired" is not particularly German) is quite different; it sardonically mocks the behavior of people living in a boardinghouse and taking "the cure." Like future stories, these begin in the middle of the action, taking it for granted that the reader will soon understand the setting. The characters still have abstract names, because they represent types, not individuals. The stories are almost entirely dialogue, interspersed with detailed descriptions of the boarders, their gestures, and, unfortunately, the overstated reactions of the first-person narrator. The plots are essentially jokes. The effect is comical but it is caricature.

The most successful, as the most genuinely amusing, is "Germans at Meat." In this story, which became the first one of *In a German Pension*, the antagonism between Germany and England is immediately brought to light. The English girl narrator is implicitly attacked (as the representative of her nation) for huge breakfasts, small families, bad tea, and fear of a German invasion. Her observations of the enormous quantity of food consumed at the German table, of the preoccupation with internal physical processes (which she prudishly wards off by clever vaudeville-style interruptions), and of the grotesquely misinformed chauvinism would provide her with a subtle victory. But she spoils the satire by her intrusive comments: "I felt I was bearing the burden of the nation's preposterous breakfast—I who drank a cup of coffee while buttoning my blouse in the morning," and "He fixed his cold blue eyes upon me with an expression which suggested a thousand premeditated invasions," when Herr Rat (the name must have been chosen with delight) challenges her teamaking ability. After Fraulein Steigelauer says the doctor has advised fruit for her health, "she very obviously followed the advice." Even worse is the girl's overt challenge, for she must stoutly sit "upright" and announce for England, "I assure you we are not afraid," and "We certainly do not want Germany." Then too, though the image is amusing, since Herr Rat did tuck his napkin into his collar, it is hard to understand why "he turned up his eyes and his moustache, wiping the soup dripping from his coat and waistcoat." The comedy seems overdone again when Herr Hoffman, "prompted by the thought" of his enjoyable sweating, "wiped his neck and face with his dinner napkin and carefully cleaned his ears." Surely this is humor on the Laurel and Hardy level.

The opening of "The Baron" involves two self-conscious observations and one sardonic remark (not understood by the dense German lady addressed) by the English girl, before it shifts momentarily to implied humor: The Frau Oberregierungsrat laments, "My omelette is empty—*empty*, and this is the third I have tried." Excessive comment and exaggeration continue to dissipate what could have been clever intimations:

[The postman] threw my letters into my milk pudding, and then turned to a waitress and whispered. She retired hastily. The manager of the pension came in with a little tray. A picture postcard was deposited on it, and reverently bowing his head, the manager of the pension carried it to the Baron.

Myself, I felt disappointed that there was not a salute of twenty-five guns.

The subject mocked is snobbery, as the pensioners speculate about and admire the aloof habits of their silent Baron. The English girl must to some extent share that snobbery since her wish-fulfillment victory this time consists of their wonder when she comes home under the Baron's umbrella. Though she mocks, she is as curious as the rest; so surely she too is deflated upon learning that his interesting habits reflect distrust of the servants and his greedy desire for double portions of food. Her ironic ending belongs to the schoolgirl: "Sic transit gloria German mundi." In fact she found it in her adolescent reading of Marie Bashkirtseff.[12]

"The Luft Bad," if the first sentence were in the past tense so as to agree with the change of attitude in the ending, would have the technical balance of "The Child-Who-Was-Tired." It consists almost entirely of banal conversation and the progressive withdrawal of the narrator from Hungarians and Russians as well as Germans. She now denies that she is either American or English, but she is told: "You must be one of the two: you cannot help it." The subject is a sardonic change of attitude. In one day the value of an umbrella is learned: it helps one to avoid the conversation of one's fellow sunbathers. The repeated themes of self-consciousness about her bare legs and speculation about umbrellas unify this tightly built but trivial story.

III

"The Luft Bad," though slight, marks a new approach in Miss Mansfield's work: the protagonist moves through a tenuous chain of experiences and undergoes a minute development of awareness. Essentially the substance of one type of Chekhov story, it also becomes part of the Mansfield stock in trade. She explores this structure in her July stories, "At Lehmann's" and "Frau Brechenmacher Attends a Wedding." But for August she has surely reverted to the superficialities of her Bavarian journal. If the *New Age* editor had observed her shift in manner, he did not apparently encourage it.

"At Lehmann's" unfolds the sexual awakening of the innocent young hotel waitress, Sabina. Contrapuntally, as "the Young Man" customer in two visits arouses her animal instincts, Frau Lehmann, swollen and unappetizing, suffers in labor. The ignorant girl knows that to have a baby requires a husband, but she wonders, "what had the man got to do with it." When she first feels drawn to the Young Man—"She wanted to look at him again—there was something about him, in his deep voice, even in the way his clothes fitted"—she is immediately aware of "the heavy dragging sound of Frau Lehmann's footsteps." This rhythmic alternation of emphasis, first used in "The Child-Who-Was-Tired," defines the form of the story. "Ugly—ugly—ugly," Sabina mutters, returning from an errand for the self-pitying Frau to the Young Man. That night in bed, made aware of her body by the Young Man's picture of a nude woman, she longs for a mirror and hugs "her little body," immediately thinking "I wouldn't be the Frau for one hundred marks—not for a thousand marks. To look like that."

All the next day Sabina's work in the café is accompanied by the groans of the woman in labor, gradually confirming the girl's rejection of such experience: " 'I think no more of it. I listen no more. Ach, I would like to go away—I hate this talk. I will not hear it. No, it is too much.' . . . But the outer door suddenly opening, she sprang to her feet and laughed. It was the Young Man again. . . . She felt better, and quite happy again." So the see-saw of feeling continues. She is frightened but does not reject his kiss in the cloakroom. Then, as he embraces her, there is a "frightful, tearing shriek," and Sabina, hearing the cry of a baby, shrieks too and rushes from the room in a final revulsion.

The more ambitious "Frau Brechenmacher Attends a Wedding" is, in several respects, like "At Lehmann's." Both stories open with a short sentence which begins the action and locates the point of view within the consciousness of the main character. (Almost immediately in the former, as though the writer were practicing already for the virtuosity of "The Daughters of the Late Colonel," there is a successfully handled, brief shift of viewpoint to the child Rosa, which unfortunately serves no function

at all.) Frau Brechenmacher, mother of five, would also like to
avoid sexual relations, but her husband, recalling with amuse-
ment her innocence and resistance on their wedding night, is unaware of her reluctance. Here is the first Mansfield characterization of the self-centered, crude family man whose overwhelming
maleness drains the life of his women. He will shortly be further
defined as Andreas Binzer, will evolve through a long line of pro-
totypes to Stanley Burnell, and will end in a final denunciation
as the self-pitying boss of "The Fly."

The full scene necessary for the wedding in "Frau Brechenmacher . . ." demands an extended technical effort. On the way
to the wedding Miss Mansfield abandons her limited viewpoint
for comments more in the style of her favorite pensioner. She
cannot resist denouncing in her own voice first the landlord of
the Gasthaus who bullies the waitresses and then Herr Brechenmacher himself. He, "completely overawed, . . . so far forgot his
rights as a husband as to beg his wife's pardon for jostling her
against the banisters in his efforts to get ahead of everybody
else." Control and the Frau's viewpoint are regained as she
listens to the guests' spiteful and gossipy conversation, reminiscent
again of the German boardinghouse. Her feelings fluctuate but
sometimes the material is so raggedly controlled that the author
seems to have forgotten where her sympathies lie: surprising
non sequiturs appear.

Everybody was laughing and talking, shaking hands, clinking glasses,
stamping on the floor—a stench of beer and perspiration filled the air.

Frau Brechenmacher, following her man down the room . . . , knew
that she was going to enjoy herself. She seemed to fill out and become
rosy and warm as she sniffed that familiar festive smell.[13]

But essentially Frau Brechenmacher responds to her environment like Miss Mansfield's *pension* persona. She sympathizes
with the reluctant, uneasy bride. When her husband presents the
newlyweds with the group's present, a silver coffeepot which is
opened to reveal the usual comment about having children, the
bride screams. The groom is amused and exposes the joke to the
laughing guests. But Frau Brechenmacher feels herself derided:
"She imagined that all these people were laughing at her, more

people than there were in the room even—all laughing at her because they were so much stronger than she was." This response and her image of the bride as "an iced cake all ready to be cut and served in neat little pieces to the bridegroom beside her" prepare the reader for a climactic gesture of pained withdrawal. Walking home and preparing supper, the Frau has asked herself repeatedly the unanswerable question, "What is it all for?" Before going to bed she concludes, "Always the same . . . but, God in heaven—how *stupid*." Then, as she lies in bed and her drunken husband lurches forward, "she put her arm across her face like a child who expected to be hurt."

This closing penetrates the mask of Katherine Mansfield. The tone agrees with that of her journal entry of June, 1909, probably written in Bavaria.[14] There after recording her pain, cold, and confusion of body, she longs for the comfort of childhood: "The only adorable thing I can imagine is for my Grandmother to put me to bed and bring me a bowl of hot milk and bread, and . . . say . . . : 'There, darling, isn't that nice?' Oh, what a miracle of happiness that would be." [15] Her latent, wistful image of herself as an injured, comfortless child accounts for her sensitive preoccupation in so many early stories with overworked or mistreated children: Rosa, the daughter of Frau Brechenmacher, who in her determined, secret mind is kin to Helen of "New Dresses"; Pearl Button; "The Little Girl"; "The Child-Who-Was-Tired"; and the child of "The Woman at the Store." Gradually these children must grow up into innocent but still tired, overworked, somehow menaced young girls like Sabina and later "The Little Governess" or the innocent of "Something Childish." Miss Mansfield's poetry of that time is also full of children, but the poems were not offered to the callous *New Age,* and the mask is secure again in the stories published in August.

"The Sister of the Baroness" is a companion piece to "The Baron," paralleling it in both theme and amateurish technique. The subject is again snobbery, but this time the Germans spend their admiration not on a greedy nobleman but on a masquerading young girl, the daughter of a dressmaker. Where in the earlier story only the narrator learned of the clay feet, in this story all are disabused in an ending as swift as that of "At Lehmann's."

But this ending is followed by an anticlimactic summary statement like that of "The Baron": "Tableau grandissimo!"—again very school-girlish.

Meanwhile, the narrator has once more overdone the caricature and overasserted her contempt for German aristocracy and romanticism. A poet allows "his tie to absorb most of his coffee" while he stares soulfully at the noble ladies. The narrator thinks "Death spasms of his Odes to Solitude! . . . from that moment his suffering temperament took up its bed and walked." Of his poem to the young girl, the narrator says: "Nine verses equally lovely commanded her to equally violent action. I am certain that had she followed his advice not even the remainder of her life in a convent would have given her time to recover her breath." On the typical German student a final aphorism is framed: "He had hitherto relied upon three scars and a ribbon to produce an effect. . . ." Gossip, snobbery, and greed are all challenged in one efficient breakfast image: "Anecdotes of the High Born were poured out, sweetened, and sipped: we gorged on scandals of High Birth generously buttered." And romance is disposed of when the German student whispers, "How I should adore to kiss you. But you know I am suffering from severe nasal catarrh. . . ." This admission is enough, but the narrator hears more: "Sixteen times last night did I count myself sneezing. And three different handkerchiefs." The eavesdropper expresses her feeling by throwing her volume of Mörike's romantic lyrics into the lilac bush.

In "Frau Fischer," as in "The Luft Bad," the narrator rejects German society, this time in the shape of aggressive advances by a widow who warns her, "When I meet new people I squeeze them dry like a sponge." The narrator thinks of wisecracks and self-consciously congratulates herself on her forbearance in not making them, but, of course, the reader has benefited, though the Germans have not. The music hall comic's trick of contrasting banal, practical conversation with lofty literature is employed, as excerpts from the "Miracles of Lourdes" are interrupted by details of preparation of the rooms Frau Fischer has engaged, until "Not even the white roses upon the feet of the Virgin could flourish in that atmosphere." [16] An almost Gogolesque comedy appears in a recollection of Herr Rat's Mack Sennett-like adventure in Turkey "with a drunken guide who was bitten by a mad dog and fell over a precipice into a field of attar of roses."

The impossibility of English-German rapport is analyzed by Frau Fischer: "Ah, that is so strange about you English. You do not seem to enjoy discussing the functions of the body. . . . How can we hope to understand anybody, knowing nothing of their stomachs?" So by implication one of the major protests of *In a German Pension* is inversely crystallized. In this story the narrator also argues more insistently than usual about waiters and marital relations and is finally goaded into asserting, "I consider child-bearing the most ignominious of all professions." [17]

The technical unity of the sketch is effected by the word *squeeze.* The squeezing promised by Frau Fischer has failed consistently. The last sentence then is obviously clever: "She squeezed my hand, but I didn't squeeze back."

IV

After a lapse of eight months, broken only by the December appearance of "A Fairy Story" in *The Open Window,* Miss Mansfield's work again began to appear in the *New Age.* Of the five stories printed between May and September of 1911, only two, "A Birthday" and "A Modern Soul," were collected for *In a German Pension.*[18] Only "A Birthday" suggests that Miss Mansfield is developing as a writer. The others are in the manner of her usual *New Age* pieces.

In a fashion, "A Birthday" takes up, again "offstage," the action of "At Lehmann's": a woman is in painful labor during the time of the story and finally gives birth to a child. A young maid is present, again innocently curious and finally in "full loathing of menkind [*sic*], vowing herself to sterility." These attitudes are akin to the sentiments of Sabina; this time they are asserted, however, with a comic effect that is out of keeping with the tone and intention of the story, which is, in fact, focused on Andreas Binzer.

The dissection of the man who is sensitive only to his own sensitivity is Miss Mansfield's purpose, and, as in many later instances, she realizes that the knife is best wielded by the individual who deserves it. Unerringly the details of Binzer's day assail his self-pitying nerves, to damn him in the reader's eyes by the time his son is born. He takes it as a matter of course that his wife will climb a rickety ladder upon which he does not care to trust himself. He makes no connection between her loss of youth since their marriage and her "three children in four years, thrown in with the dusting, so to speak," as the doctor reminds him. He regrets that he has gone out without breakfast to get this doctor for his wife, and he is in many ways annoyed by the man's competent, realistic conversation. The maid, too, makes him fear for his health when she spits on his shoe before shining it, and she nearly ruins his very hearty breakfast by not appearing promptly with a warm plate for the fish. It is annoying also that his Sunday must be spoiled by the absence of the children and by the inattentiveness of his wife on this occasion. And the wind, that New Zealand wind [19] which will rise to similar effect again in "The Wind Blows," unnerves him further.

But this is not caricature. There is tenderness too in Andreas Binzer; it is aroused by the sound of church bells and by resulting memories of other Sunday mornings with his wife. He looks at and even kisses her photograph. At that moment her cry is heard and, like Sabina's in "At Lehmann's," his feeling changes. Her photographic smile becomes "secret, even cruel," and he comes close to destroying the picture. This sequence, as well as his previous meditation about developing his business for the boy whose birth he awaits, clearly foreshadows "The Fly." The interlude has displayed a new depth of perception in the author, but no lack of conviction about the dominant nature of Binzer. His moment of terror—when the wind dies and the house is suddenly silent—he would express in the self-pitying, sentimental words, "My beloved wife has passed away!" Instead he learns that the son has indeed been born. He triumphantly sums up his day: "Well, by God! Nobody can accuse *me* of not knowing what suffering is." It is a fitting conclusion from Miss Mansfield's first fallible narrator.

The other three stories are marked by the flaws of her earliest attempts with the *pension* guests. The same excessively sardonic narrator caricatures too much. The comedy is often slapstick— what better subject than German boarders giving a benefit performance for afflicted infants, as in "The Modern Soul"? But "The Journey to Bruges" and "A Truthful Adventure" have abandoned the Germans to express a more general contempt for humanity. In the latter the narrator, shamelessly identified now as "Katherine," is opposed to everything which crosses her path. Ladies, servants, painters, boatmen, an old school friend from New Zealand, guidebooks, and women's suffrage, even Bruges itself, shrivel before her disaffected eye. This story also boasts probably the worst sentence Miss Mansfield ever wrote: "One cannot expect to travel in upholstered boats with people who are enlightened enough to understand laughter that has its wellsprings in sympathy."

In March of the following year two more Mansfield pieces appeared, so poor that neither she nor even Murry ever cared to reprint them. In two years, of the sixteen stories and sketches Miss Mansfield wrote for the *New Age,* only four, and one of these the derivative "The Child-Who-Was-Tired," manifest the degree of control and perception that forecast work of literary value. The others display only the sort of competence with witty phrase and situation which might today sustain, for a season, a second-rate comedy series for television. Apparently, despite her grateful letter to Orage in later years, the taste of the *New Age* was not demanding; its influence was not, therefore, destined to elicit excellence from Katherine Mansfield.

Three more stories, not published before, appeared in *In a German Pension.* "The Advanced Lady," which takes place in the *pension,* is in the manner of the other stories set there, but "The Swing of the Pendulum" and "A Blaze" strike a new note. If the women of the German boardinghouse have flirted, they have done so decorously. These two stories, though a slight attempt is made in the names of the characters to relate them to a German scene, suggest rather experiments at living in an English Bohemia. In both a woman toys briefly with the affections of a man, recoils, and returns to an earlier male tie.

Viola of "The Swing of the Pendulum" is an innocent girl, who daydreams like Rosabel; battles her surprising wooer, though with greater vigor, as "The Little Governess" will; and foreshadows in several respects Ada Moss of "Pictures." Viola's swing of feeling from the apparently faithful though poverty-stricken lover, Casimir, to the well-to-do, idle, sensual stranger, and back from the aggressive attentions of the stranger to Casimir, belongs entirely to an unreal world. Even her room is dingy poverty one moment, the lair of a great courtesan the next. It is the older, defeated artist, Miss Moss, who is really compelled to confront in the more mature story the solution to poverty that youthful Viola merely toys with.

In "A Blaze" Elsa, catlike in her desire for admiration, causes the "blaze" quite knowingly, but she is equally withdrawn from the dangers of her flirtation. Almost entirely in dialogue, the story is one of the few which makes no use of a viewpoint character. The only hint of the author's meaning rests in the ironies implicit in the somewhat deceived husband's final appraisal: "God! What a woman you are."

The stories collected for *In a German Pension*—published in December, 1911—announce themes and techniques which were to become permanent characteristics of Miss Mansfield's writing. Though she has not yet identified the scene, she has begun to exploit her New Zealand materials. Her focus is entirely personal, but she is developing from sardonic bitter rejection toward the mingling of compassion with criticism. Already ill-health has begun her years of isolated subjugation to strangers in foreign boardinghouses and hotels; she will never cease to reject these people—with violence in her correspondence,[20] with mounting restraint in her stories. Her exploration of sexual relationships is bluntly begun, but it will become more penetrating, yet more tentative, as she matures. She has already introduced most of her characters: mistreated children; innocent but exploring young girls; garrulous, overbearing single or widowed women; downtrodden, physically wasted wives; and overbearing self-satisfied husbands. No story has yet focused on a young man, though such an abstract figure provides a sounding board for the experimental young woman of "A Blaze" and waits in the wings, motivating "The Swing of the Pendulum."

Technically, Miss Mansfield has found but perhaps has not recognized the form which will best convey her experience. Her stories already begin with little or no introduction of character or scene, usually in the mind of a central figure. She has found a fallible narrator only once, in Andreas Binzer. The physical action, if any (it may be taking place upstairs, offstage), consists of blows to the sensibility. In the poorer German *pension* stories, this sensibility is static; it merely announces the author's repugnance. The excessively caustic caricatures reflect her immaturity. The stories, however, have technical balance.

In those few stories which promise the future Katherine Mansfield the purpose is discovery: a shift in awareness; an enlargement of self-knowledge; or, more subtly, an available self-knowledge, rejected by the central character but known by the author and the reader who have followed the progress of this developing consciousness. The irony of such observations is mellowed and strengthened as the young writer learns not to state her conclusion overtly.

Though *In a German Pension* was enthusiastically reviewed,[21] Miss Mansfield was nearly finished, for a time, with writing for the *New Age,* which had spawned ten of the stories.

CHAPTER 3

Three Little Magazines

I

IN DECEMBER, 1911, Katherine Mansfield received an encouraging rejection slip from John Middleton Murry, the young editor of a new publication, *Rhythm*. She had sent him a "fairy tale," but the aim of *Rhythm*, announced in the first number, was to reject aestheticism and its limited, if exquisite, vision. Instead, the editors cried for "an art that strikes deeper . . . drawing its inspiration from aversion, to a deeper and a broader field . . . in its pity and its brutality it shall be real." Miss Mansfield immediately provided what was required in "The Woman at the Store," [1] and Murry hailed it as "by far the best story that had been sent to *Rhythm*."

For the scene of this story Miss Mansfield drew on her memories of the New Zealand back country. The frontier store and the hot, raw, isolated countryside are described in painstaking detail. Dialect is imitated in the speech of the characters, and several of the words employed—*whare, wideawake, milkbilly, sundowners* —need glossing. With this naturalistic technique is blended the brutal subject of murder and insanity.

The carefully plotted story is traditional in its form. The opening appearance of the woman carrying a rifle neatly foreshadows the drawing by the child which reveals the murder. Jo's casual, drunken remark, "No good cryin' over spilt 'usbands!" provides a similar irony, as does the woman's deceptive "if I was a secret woman I'd place any confidence in your 'ands." The repeated question concerning the husband's whereabouts and the child's threat to draw a forbidden picture lead easily to the dénouement. But the attempt at the end to weight the significance of the discovery results in very unnatural behavior. After the long, exhausting day's ride, the narrator writes: "Jim and I sat till dawn with the drawing beside us."

Thus the narrator-participant avoids comment on the crucial event. However, she does remark, upon observing the woman, her child, and the store, "Good Lord, what a life!" A trace of the supercilious German *pension* style intrudes while the narrator is drinking with Jo and the woman: "He reached his hand across the table and held hers, and though the position looked most uncomfortable when they wanted to pass the water and whisky, their hands stuck together as though glued."

It is the effect of isolation and a hard life on the woman which interests Miss Mansfield, rather than the plot of detection. In a central passage the woman utters sentiments akin to those of Frau Brechenmacher; speaking of past conversations with her husband, she says: "Over and over I tells 'im—you've broken my spirit and spoiled my looks, and wot for—that's wot I'm driving at. . . . Oh, some days—an' months of them—I 'ear them two words knockin' inside me all the time—'Wot for!' but sometimes I'll be cooking the spuds an' I lifts the lid off to give 'em a prong and I 'ears, quite sudden again, 'Wot for!' " (The accuracy yet inconsistency with which Miss Mansfield recorded the back country dialect is evident.)

By the time the spring issue of *Rhythm* appeared, not only did this story and two Mansfield poems masquerading as translations of "Boris Petrovsky" occupy the lion's share of the magazine, but Katherine and Murry had met and their relationship was moving swiftly toward erratic permanence. On April 11, 1912, for seven and six a week, Murry took lodgings in the "music room" of Miss Mansfield's flat, a purely business arrangement to help Murry move away from home. Though Murry's account makes it seem that they lodged for a long time under the same roof like friendly, intellectual brothers, within a month they slept together and went happily to Paris to obtain J. D. Fergusson's blessing upon their union.[2]

Thus with the June issue (already a financial failure, *Rhythm* now changed publishers and irrationally became a monthly) the lion became one of a pair of Tigers, as Miss Mansfield and Murry announced "The Meaning of Rhythm." For the first time there was a masthead, listing Murry as editor "Assisted by: Katherine Mansfield and Michael T. H. Sadleir." The next month Sadleir's name was gone. Despite denunciations from the *New Age*, which in June printed its last Mansfield piece for three years, *Rhythm* continued through March, 1913. In May it became for three monthly issues the *Blue Review;* then it vanished from the literary scene. Miss Mansfield also vanished from publication until she and Murry became involved during the fall of 1915 with the D. H. Lawrence-inspired *Signature*, a thin magazine which saw three issues in one month and then was done, having printed only the works of its three founders.

During these three and a half years Katherine Mansfield spent her energies on poetry, stories, critical articles, and reviews, as well as on the business affairs of the three little magazines edited by Murry. To help finance them, she sacrificed her annual allowance from her father. She supported herself by entertaining with comic songs or monologues at Mayfair tea parties and by acting as an extra in silent movies.[3] She published fourteen stories in these periodicals and one in Frank Harris's *House and Home*. Inevitably she heard during this time a tremendous amount of talk about art. Restlessly she participated in it. But her own writing for these magazines exhibited little advance beyond her earlier work.

The noncritical writing begins in August and September with two false starts which have never been collected. Apparently attempts in the Russian manner, these stories are presumably supposed to be brutal—as the magazine required. "Tales of a Courtyard" consists of three sketches connected only by the cold setting. One begins with a first-person plural viewpoint, as dwellers in the courtyard rejoice in the coming of spring, but, when they jeer at the outsider inmate, a Russian girl, the author has abandoned the original point of view. The fluctuation of emotion from pleasure through speculation to gloom and final derision is handled with economy. It is a description of the "democratic mob" scorned by the aristocratic artists of "Seriousness in Art."

Sketch two, "The Following After" has a dreamlike, feverish quality as a girl seeks Mark, who has angrily left her to "end the whole bloody business." Eventually she follows what may be his *revenant* to a room where he lies stiffly. Her mental state has been suggested somewhat in the manner of "The Child-Who-Was-Tired"; it is similarly hallucinatory from weariness, but is conveyed through intensely perceived color images (yellow street lights on white snow) which suggest that Miss Mansfield's association with the Fauvist painters encouraged by *Rhythm* is intensifying her visual imagery. The sketch concludes with a typically ambiguous but "brutal" image: "She was so tired that for a moment she thought it was the sunrise staining the pillow so red."

In the third sketch, "By Moonlight," Feodor sits on a snowy bench beside an old man who delights in a precious, beautiful book, which he will not sell despite his poverty. When he sleeps, Feodor steals it, suffers from conscience through the night, determines to return the book but does not. In the morning the old man is found dead on the cold bench. The influence on plot and psychology is apparently that of Dostoyevsky, in a very much diluted fashion.

"Spring in a Dream," the attempt of the following month, is Russian only in the names of the characters. More pity than brutality is displayed for the young cripple Michael, the recipient of inadequate sympathy from his relatives, who prefer the memory of his active, revolutionary youth. The center of interest lies in the increase of depth in the viewpoint character from "he ought to realize that we have so short a holiday at home and no time to be eternally sympathetic," to her final perception of Michael weeping at his loss of strength: "And now the sun, shining through the front windows, painted on the bare floor the shadow of Michael with his lap full of fruit." This shadow, juxtaposing the broken man with the fulfillment of harvested fruit, gains in blunt strength in contrast to the fragile opening image of the story, a shadow of chrysanthemums "too delicate and fine for the heavy room. . . . It quivered as though longing to go back and hide among the petals of the plants," causing the viewpoint character to speculate on "the terror of captive shadow." Again the work is strongly visual, but it manages through implication to convey compassionate irony. Perhaps the author is now looking at *Rhythm* reproductions of the refined, early drawings of Picasso rather than the stark, Fauvist decorations Anne Estelle Rice made for the magazine.

In the same issue appeared "How Pearl Button Was Kidnapped," an earlier work according to Murry's pre-*New Age* date of 1910. This wish-fulfillment account of a child stolen by gypsies rejects the ordinary conventional life from which *Rhythm*, despite its slogan of realism, recoils. Pearl innocently asks the gypsies: "Don't you all live in a row? Don't the men go to offices? Aren't there any nasty things?" But the police come running toward her across the seashore just as she has become ecstatically happy, "a crowd of little blue men to carry her back to the House of Boxes." The entire story is seen from the viewpoint of a very young child. To create the impression of utter simplicity, Miss Mansfield experiments in parataxis very successfully. It recurs in "Something Childish But Very Natural"; however, in her later portraits of children she never used the technique again, perhaps because the children were never again so innocent.

Elena, the child of "New Dresses," is a determined, rebellious, persecuted child. "Hellish!" she shouts, describing her environment to the sympathetic Doctor Erb.[4] Though the plot concerns the conflict of Elena with her parents, focused in her childish attempt to conceal the tearing of her new dress, the author's interest is diffused. A series of four episodes covering three days comments largely on the characters and relationships of the adults. Andreas Binzer, the father, is still parsimonious, inconsiderate, self-centered, and self-pitying. He is so "overcome" by Elena's stolid indifference to his appeals that he puts his outdoor boots on the starched bolster of his bed. His wife, very antagonistic to Elena, weeps at the story of her misbehavior. Her attitude fluctuates between resentment at her husband's attempts at economy (which she actually ignores) and appreciation of his fine looks and generosity. The grandmother seems to dote a little. Anna Binzer thinks so early in the story; the doctor, when she fails to appreciate that by recovering the dress he has saved Elena a whipping, comments, "she doesn't take in half I say." The approach in which people are revealed from a variety of shifting viewpoints and by the implications of their own actions and responses foreshadows, as do the scene and subject, "Prelude."

The last paragraph of the *Rhythm* version of "New Dresses" has been wisely excluded from the Murry edition. It followed Miss Mansfield's early usual technique of unification, through the repetition of opening images about the dresses, deepened by other remarks which recall the themes of Elena's rebellion and her mother's extravagant indifference. The artifice is unnecessary to finish a story which, having opened in the middle of an environment where all is assumed to be familiar to the reader, should properly close on the musing evaluative comment of the doctor,

[45]

returning the emphasis to the lack of adult understanding of a child's world.

As in the spring, Miss Mansfield is again filling an issue, for she supplies in this one of October another story and a sketch. "The Little Girl" plays an odd counterpoint to a story by Murry, "The Little Boy," printed in August. Murry's story draws on childhood memory, brutalized, presumably to conform to *Rhythm* policy. It details the agony of a six-year-old in the care of a hag who beats him often with a leather strap. He fears alleys and corners, has nightmares over the decorations of a Christmas paper. Terrified, he apparently breaks his leg on the way to the old woman's room, where he wants to climb into her bed for comfort. She strikes him, and he crawls painfully down to the cellar and is left anticipating death with the rats.[5]

In "The Little Girl," Kass, renamed Kezia in Murry's edition, is in fear, not of alleys and corners, but of her overwhelming, impatient, brusque, giantlike father. Innocently, she tears up an important speech to make him a birthday present and is whipped on her hands with a ruler. Despite her grandmother's comforting (again the mother only leads the culprit to the father), her fear is confirmed, and she first questions "What did Jesus make father's for?" Then, from watching the playful father next door, she learns there are different sorts. Left alone in the house with her father, she screams out in a nightmare, but the man takes her tenderly into bed with him, where she concludes that although he is too tired from hard work to be a playful father he has a big heart.

In contrast to Murry's pointless extravagance, Miss Mansfield's story develops a change in feeling in its viewpoint character. Except for two small lapses in her interior monologue (in reference to her stuttering, she "had quite given it up," and she watches light through venetian blinds "trace a sad little pattern"), the diction consistently maintains the child's viewpoint and the structure is formally compact. The parallels in content suggest that the story was written as a mild, realistic corrective to Murry's view.

"Sunday Lunch" is merely a *New Age*-like attack on the malice of self-satisfied, materially successful dilettantes who consider themselves artists but are "not real enough to die." [6] This sardonic tone is typical of her reviews, as when she ticks off Galsworthy's *Moods, Songs and Doggerels* with "Mr. Galworthy is wise in that he avoids all mention of the word 'poetry' in connexion with his verses." [7] This attitude contrasts strongly with Murry's typical adulation, for instance, in his extravagant praise of James Stephens and Frank Harris.[8]

"Ole Underwood" in January was the second of Miss Mansfield's efforts at local color in the New Zealand back country, and her last story for *Rhythm*. Like "The Woman at the Store" with which she began in the magazine, it is violent in content and intensely visual in the bright colors of the Post-Impressionists and Fauvists.[9] A strong wind, an intensified heartbeat, and a red-and-white handkerchief are violently interrelated images which seem to motivate Ole Underwood's reactions. Continually he sees red and his heart beats "madly." A crazy outcast, he experiences a moment of tenderness for a stray cat which recalls his faithless but beloved wife; then, in revulsion, he tosses the cat into the sewer and apparently goes on board a ship. But the ending is hallucinatory. The man on the bunk with his head on a red pillow (recalling the closing image of the second of the "Tales of a Courtyard") may be the man he killed long ago, a vision of himself long ago, or an innocent stranger whom the madman is about to kill. This deliberate ambiguity fittingly completes the portrait within the viewpont of the crazy man.

II

The *New Age* had hailed "The Woman at the Store" as "defiant of the rules of art, for it ploughs the realistic sand, with no single relief of wisdom or wit. . . ." [10] Of "Ole Underwood" it said: "Miss Mansfield makes an inartistic stink with a dirty old imbecile who murders cats." [11] But when the *Blue Review* replaced *Rhythm*, though disapproval of the publication continued—"Can the leopard change its spots?"—the *New Age* was delighted with "Pension Séguin": "the best work she has done since she left us for an editorial feather in her cap. . . . She has made amends. . . . Here is work which we are very pleased indeed to welcome." [12] The reason for such approval is obvious: in this story—and in two to follow, "Violet" and "Bains Turcs"—Miss Mansfield has returned to her German *pension* manner and is writing the type of story that the *New Age* editorial policy encouraged. The editors recognized their own when they saw it. The title under which the stories originally appeared, "Epilogues" I, II, and III, may have been intended to recall the earlier success.

Now the pressure of journalistic work appears for the first time in Miss Mansfield's letters: "Such a relief that I've written my reviews again and started my *Epilogue.*" And the next letter: "I've nursed the *Epilogue* to no purpose. Every time I pick it up and hear 'You'll keep it to six,' I can't cut it. To my knowledge there aren't any superfluous words: I mean every line of it. . . . I'd rather it wasn't there at all than sitting in the *Blue Review* with a broken nose and one ear as though it had jumped into an editorial dogfight." And the next: "P.S. I don't know whether you will roar at me, darling, for doing the books in this way. But they lent themselves to it, and I thought if you read the review you would see that it's almost silly to notice them singly and that they gain like this. If wrong, return the thing, and I'll do you two little ones." [13] She won. "Violet" (Epilogue II) remained six and a half pages and two books appeared in one review.

Of the three *New Age* style stories, only the third, "Bains Turcs," in a sudden revelation of concealed character, has a degree of depth. All are clever wit but of insignificant value. Essentially, they criticize humanity in something akin to the manner Miss Mansfield had decried in "Sunday Lunch." The one development is that, at last, the viewpoint character, so smug in *In a German Pension,* has begun to laugh at herself. As "Pension Séguin" (Epilogue I) begins, she introduces her peculiar fright upon entering the boardinghouse as "ridiculous," which it certainly is. Her immediate antagonism to the place and to the people is as unmotivated as in the earlier stories, and the fluctuation of attitude is as uncontrolled as in "Frau Brechenmacher Attends a Wedding." After a sardonic rumination on the white mats which dominate the salon, her heart "leapt up again at these signs and tokens of virtue and sobriety," and, philosophically defending her belief in appearances, she takes the room for two months. Courage has aphoristically fled "like a disobedient dog." Contrary to expectation the place is a bedlam, M. Séguin looks like a rat, the most wicked of the badly behaved children is significantly named Hélène, and the conversation is banal. The climax exposes her belief in appearances: the mats were made by the lady on the first floor. Miss Mansfield has returned to the Chekhovian joke pattern.

"Violet" continues at the *pension*, opening with the awakening of the self-conscious pensioner who admires her own fanciful imagery in the manner of the later Raoul Duquette. She imagines herself defending the truth of proverbs, be they ever so unctuous and irritating, against Katherine Tynan's whimsical arguments. The pensioner looking out the window is a sentimental daydreamer, awakened to reality by a servant beating rugs. She knows her sober breakfast reflections are both "pious and smug." Then, as in "A Truthful Adventure," comes the chance meeting with an old friend, Violet, who has a romantic secret to reveal. Delayed by the witty oppositions of the pensioner, who admits "I did not know how to sympathize," Violet finally reveals that her experience of the "pinnacles . . . and depths" consists of her recent seven dances, long talk, and final kiss from a man who immediately confessed that he was engaged. "Is that all?" cried the letdown auditor, and knows that the sound of the fountain "half sly, half laughing" (this is a repeated image, the usual unifying trick) is laughing at her. Except for consistent self-mockery, there is no necessary relationship between the beginning and the end. Perhaps the story could not have been cut by one half page, but it could have been split in two.

"Bains Turcs" (Epilogue III) has the natural unity of consisting entirely of observations which could have been and probably were made at a Turkish bath. They begin with the usual repugnance for ugly human beings and continue to a choice of daydreams brought on by the odors of the Warm Room. Mockery of the other inmates is voiced in the amused conversation of two stout blondes, who are especially entertained by the inability of a German, named, for the nonce, Mackintosh Cap, to get service from the French attendant. Although the German-speaking, French-speaking viewpoint character could have helped her but did not, Mackintosh Cap begins a conversation in the Hot Room. She wants a sympathetic hearer; though the pensioner is withdrawn, Mackintosh Cap thinks she has one simply because the language barrier is broken. She denounces the attendant and is resolved not to tip in this "scandalous place." She recognizes that the blondes are "not respectable women—you can tell at a glance." Their insulting laughter has ruined her sweat. She also manages to mention modesty, domestic duties, and her five children, one born dead, all produced in six years of marriage. Most of what Katherine Mansfield dislikes about the Germans has been epitomized in this "ugly, wretched figure . . . railing against the two fresh beauties." In the anteroom as all depart, the blondes are indeed attractive in "charming feathered hats and furs" as opposed to the German woman's "terrible bird nest . . . *Reise-hut.*" But there is effected a brilliantly swift turn of impression. Mackintosh Cap comments, "How do you suppose they can afford clothes like that? The horrible low creatures. No, they're enough to make a young girl think twice." Then she "stared after them, her sallow face all mouth and eyes, like the face of a hungry child before a forbidden table." And in this closing Miss Mansfield has finally reached her top pitch in achieving the objectives of *Rhythm:* a brutal analysis of the woman's motive for her calumniations, inextricably blended with a sudden flash of insight and consequent pity.

It has become customary to treat the three stories of New Zealand low life together, despite chronology, merely because they treat similar subjects and are essentially untypical of Miss Mansfield's work. However, in terms of technique "Millie" is more akin to "Bains Turcs," with the same sudden turn of awareness and penetration into human complexity at the end. Millie seems to be a hard, ignorant, crude woman. Willfully childless, she is unexpectedly moved when she finds an injured young man behind the woodpile. A "strange, dreadful feeling . . . some seed that had never flourished . . . unfolded and struck deep roots and burst into painful leaf." Realizing that he is the murderer that her husband and other men are away looking for, she determines to help him because "Men is all beasts" but " 'E's nothink but a sick kid."

That night, after the men have returned and are in bed, she lies rigid, hoping the young man will now escape: "I don' care anythink about justice an' all the rot they've bin spoutin' to-night. . . . 'Ow are yer to know what anythink's like till yer *do* know? It's all rot." The question bears ironically on her own lack of self-knowledge, for she is to take a second unexpected turn. When the dog barks and pursuit begins again, first she is horrified; but then "a strange mad joy smothered everything else. She rushed into the road—she laughed and shrieked and danced in the dust, jigging the lantern. 'A—ah! Arter 'im, Sid! A—a—a—h! Ketch him, Willie. Go it! Go it! A—ah, Sid! Shoot 'im down. Shoot 'im down. Shoot 'im!' " This is the only backwoods story in which complexity of character is examined.

In this sudden onset of bloodlust there is a raw kinship with Viola of "The Swing of the Pendulum." One moment she is playing the childish game of charades with a strange man; in the next, fighting him off, she bites him and rejoices at his pain. Feeling a "glorious, intoxicating happiness" at the fray, she then becomes again her sentimental self. The feeling is related too to that of the *Scrapbook* Kezia of 1916 who smiles, though also still frightened, remembering that on the previous evening, standing up to her father for the first time, she called him "Bottlenose." [14] The violence of Matilda in the *Signature* "Autumn II" was not modified five years later when the story was rewritten slightly as "The Wind Blows" for the *Athenaeum*. Matilda, defying her mother and full of fury still rushes out into the wind shouting "Go to hell." Though her expressions became tamer, Miss Mansfield did not lose interest in latent human violence. Many of her stories study cruelty and its effects until, in the end, "The Fly" offers an overwhelming analysis of the impulse.

III

When the *Blue Review* failed in July, Katherine Mansfield suffered a creative lull. She would not publish again until the October and November 1915 issues of the *Signature*. In December she and Murry moved to Paris where they were able to stay till the end of February. While there she wrote "Something Childish But Very Natural," not published until 1924. This story, with "An Indiscreet Journey" and a first draft beginning of "The Aloe," fills the two-year interlude before D. H. Lawrence interested Miss Mansfield and Murry in the brief-lived *Signature*.

For the moment not writing for any magazine, limited neither by the demands of space nor editorial policy, Katherine Mansfield produced a story more than twice as long as her usual one, and far more carefully wrought. She replaced the sudden flash of insight exposed in an unexpected final image, with the detailed development of sensitively perceived feeling. Her very different purpose is that the reader should come to know and understand the innocent longing, sweetness, and pain of an adolescent love affair. It was hardly calculated to appeal to her literary friends and was not published until after her death.

Her evaluative challenge lies in the title—"Something Childish But Very Natural." It was childish of Edna to withdraw so repeatedly from Henry's chaste advances, but because she was sixteen it was also natural. It was childish, too, of seventeen-year-old Henry to arrange, in his longing, to play house with Edna, but again, very natural. Their whole delicate, fanciful love affair was childish, an affair truly of children, but it was as natural as any of the more violent deterministic outpourings of the naturalistic school, perhaps more natural, and certainly built to convey a tenderer sympathy.

The tale seems deceptively simple at first. It moves straightforwardly through the initial meeting of the pair, a few typical encounters, and the two fresh childlike love letters, to the day when Edna fails to come to the cottage Henry has rented. But the design pronounces this more than a disaster of childhood; it is a failure of faith. Though she handles the story entirely from Henry's point of view, Miss Mansfield takes particular care that Edna, who fails, shall be understood. At that second meeting on the train Edna sits stiffly; her hands tremble; she won't let Henry touch her hair and moves "a little away from him" in a dark tunnel. In the concert hall she won't let Henry help her with her coat and insists on holding the program to read to herself. Henry wonders,

Why did he want to touch her so much and why did she mind? Whenever he was with her he wanted to hold her hand or take her arm when they walked together, or lean against her—not hard—just lean lightly so that his shoulder should touch her shoulder—and she wouldn't even have that. All the time that he was away from her he was hungry, he craved the nearness of her. There seemed to be comfort and warmth breathing from Edna that he needed to keep him calm. Yes, that was it. He couldn't get calm with her because she wouldn't let him touch her.

Here is natural passion registered on an innocent mind.

Edna sees him brooding and promises to "explain something" after the concert, but she loses her nerve for a moment, foreshadowing her later dereliction, and tries to leave him. Then she recovers the courage to try to explain. She is aware that her evasions are hurting Henry, but, naturally, she cannot help it: "It's not that I'm frightened of you—it's not that—it's only a feeling, Henry, that I can't understand myself even. . . . Somehow I feel if once we did that—you know—held each other's hands and kissed it would be all changed. . . . We wouldn't be children any more . . . silly, isn't it?" While she speaks, "behind her as in a dream he saw the sky and half a white moon and the trees of the square with their unbroken buds"—images which confirm her remarks. At this point Henry promises to "bury the bogy in this square," and they begin a childish but natural attempt to live unnaturally, as if they were, indeed, in a dream.

"London became their playground." Sentence rhythm and repetitions reinforce the childlike pretense of their activities: "They found their own shops . . . and their own tea-shop with their own table—their own streets—and one night . . . they found their own village." Everything is fancifully small: Henry expects "little low houses . . . and . . . little shops with lamps in the windows"; and he is correct. The words *little, small, tiny* repeat themselves with every new discovery. One house Henry would like to live in, and Edna agrees "with a dreamy smile." They weave a fantasy of their childlike married life in this house, even including the little cat who comes through the fence. But suddenly Henry wants to leave because "it's going to turn into a dream." He fears the dream in a very real way, for on another day, he has said to Edna, who continues to wear her "strange, dreamy smile," "Long after you have stopped laughing . . . I can hear your laugh running up and down my veins—and yet—are we a dream?"

And suddenly he saw himself and Edna as two very small children walking through the streets, looking through windows, buying things and playing with them, talking to each other, smiling . . . and then he rolled over and pressed his face in the leaves—faint with longing.

He wanted to kiss Edna, and to put his arms around her and press her to him and feel her cheek hot against his kiss and kiss her until he'd no breath left and so stifle the dream.

After tea where Henry tells the proprietor that Edna is his sister, they investigate a "tiny" cottage which is for rent. Edna leans against Henry, lets him embrace her though her voice is shaky, and finally tells him that she has "quite got over the feeling."

In the next scene Henry has rented and prepared the cottage and is waiting for Edna. "I don't believe this for a minute," he thinks, but Edna earlier has said: "You have faith, haven't you?" So now he anticipates her coming, their supper, even their going to bed, childishly, in separate rooms, for it is still only a play house. Sitting on the doorstep, he recalls her question: " 'Haven't you faith, Henry?' 'I hadn't then. Now I have,' he said, 'I feel just like God.' " There is pathetic irony in this declaration.

The climax of the story is seen like the dream he feared, for Henry falls asleep and sleepily thinks he sees a white moth coming down the road. On their second meeting, he had said to Edna, " 'I believe I've swallowed a butterfly—and it's fanning its wings just here.' He put his hand on his heart." Now the white moth becomes a little girl with a telegram. Henry remains in a dream as he speculates, "Perhaps it's only a make-believe one, and it's got one of those snakes inside it that fly up at you." Miss Mansfield does not reveal the real snake that jumped out, but the insects which symbolically suggest the state of the soul are trapped in the implied image of the final paragraph: "The garden became full of shadows—they span a web of darkness over the cottage and the trees and Henry and the telegram. But Henry did not move."

Henry, as his acquaintance with Edna began, had explained that they had found each other by being natural. He added, "That's all life is—something childish and very natural. Isn't it?" and Edna agreed. But in the end, after Henry found faith, she rejected it and returned him to the dream, which is not life and not natural. The final position of Henry, dreaming in darkness lest he awake alone, exactly echoes the second and third stanzas of the poem whence he acquired his philosophy and with which the story began:

> But in my sleep to you I fly,
> I'm always with you in my sleep,
> . . . .
> But then one wakes and where am I?
> All, all alone.
> . . . .
> For though my sleep be gone,
> Yet while 'tis dark one shuts one's lids,
> And so, dreams on.

The name of the poem is "Something Childish But Very Natural." While Henry waits for Edna, he remembers only the opening three optimistic lines:

> Had I but two little wings,
> And were a little feathery bird,
> To you I'd fly, my dear. . . . .

The rest of the stanza, "But thoughts like these are idle things,/ And I stay here," is the denial—the warning which from the beginning he has ignored.

The structure of this apparently simple story turns out to be very intricate; it is built to move the reader through an interplay of images and rhythms, and a design of ironic echoes. Miss Mansfield has taken great pains to convey, without sentimentality, an experience almost too delicate to communicate. Employing Henry's viewpoint, she maintains the necessary objectivity and control.

IV

A year passed before "An Indiscreet Journey" was composed, partly from journal entries concerning an actual wartime journey, made to visit Francis Carco in February, 1915. The journal contains parts of the middle of the story. Comparison with the finished work reveals a little of Miss Mansfield's intent as she rearranges segments, revises minute details, but maintains much of her original jaunty attitude.

The story rests its point of view in the adventurous traveler. This young woman, aware of the illegality of her projected visit into the front-line area, covers her fear with a bravado of self-mockery. The result seems to be frivolous inability to take the war seriously: the soldiers look as though they expect to be photographed. Each guard she sees as "a *petit soldat,* all boots and bayonet. Forlorn and desolate he looked,—like a little comic picture waiting for the joke to be written underneath." But with this image begins the counterpoint theme, for the passage continues: "Is there really such a thing as war? Are all those laughing voices really going to the war? These dark woods lighted so mysteriously by the white stems of the birch and the ash—these watery fields with the big birds flying over—these rivers green and blue in the light—have battles been fought in places like these?"

And she observes the "beautiful" cemeteries, gay and full of flowers she thinks at first, but no: they are ribbons tied on to soldiers' graves. It is, in fact, disbelief that her gaiety reflects. She cannot take in the reality of war, which can only appear absurd in the context of "darling" soldiers and their "ridiculous" uniforms. The officials she must delude are also ridiculous. The peak of her necessary but absurd terror is reflected in her unnerved readiness to kneel to these "sumptuous and omnipotent" men, whom she calls God I and God II.

The repeated religious imagery conveys her vision of the French at war. Opening in an observation of her concierge as St. Anne, "really very beautiful," the traveler sees herself derisively through the eyes of the calamity-predicting Frenchwoman. At a buffet where she must change trains, the humble presence of an old man with a bucket of fish, looking "as though he had escaped from some holy picture, and was entreating the soldiers' pardon for being there at all," challenges the world of war and leaves the viewpoint character with a guilty feeling that she should have bought the fish, if only to throw them away. And at the end of the story, as the customers of a café silently listen to the military police pass after closing time, "the faces lifted, listening. 'How beautiful they are!' I thought. 'They are like a family party having supper in the New Testament. . . .'" It is the beauty of these people which in every case challenges the reality of war and renders its concerns absurdly impossible.

The insistence of this imagery is intensified by several changes in tone. From the balance of terror and nervous wit in the first section, the story turns to the more realistic observation of soldiers near the front. Wounded men are seen petting a "mangy, shivering dog." In a café amid the casual complaints of soldiers and the distractions of drink and card-playing, a man sits uncontrollably weeping, his eyes just unbandaged from an injury. The man groans from time to time, but the other men, quarreling and laughing over their game, pay no attention to what is commonplace in their experience. Only the proprietress is finally compelled to comment, "*Mais vous savez, c'est un peu dégoûtant, ça,*" to which they casually agree.

The final section focuses on the intensity with which one man, "the blue-eyed soldier," insists upon finding a very special drink for the English girl. The half-drunk conversation and the trivial goal of the insistent guest which, like the girl's journey, involves an indiscreet challenging of army regulations, end the story. The group is drinking in a dirty scullery to avoid being caught by the police. But the voice of the blue-eyed soldier is happy in the dark, and he pronounces the whiskey "excellent—*ex-cellent.*" This closing on a small satisfaction is tonally controlled by the recurrent religious imagery; it recalls for the reader that—though now in the dark and pursuing small, temporary satisfactions—these people have a beauty that is somehow reminiscent of holiness.

At the time of this writing Miss Mansfield was strongly opposed to excess spirituality; however, in this story, without any overt statement, maintaining her objectivity through the consciousness of a rather frivolous yet sensitive observer, she manages to surround her soldiers with compassionate vision and thus to underline the ugly "joke" too many of them were waiting for. The action of the story, too, supports this motif. It is almost entirely taken up with alternately waiting and trying to get somewhere. There is waiting for trains, for food, for a companion, for the approval of officials, and for the police to pass. And through this waiting one sees continually soldiers and occasional civilians, all confronting the war by waiting and by passing time as if they were doing something else.

For, sitting in a café, the narrator can feel that years have passed and "Perhaps the war is long since over—there is no village outside at all—the streets are quiet under the grass," and it seems like the "very last day of all. . . ." Only the entrance of the proprietress and the soldiers brings her back to reality, which is only a waiting for another reality which she cannot experience, cannot, indeed, realize, but only somehow challenge in her view of the simplicity and beauty of these people, so absurdly, so impossibly out of place, as she is, in a wartime setting.

V

Her brother Leslie Beauchamp, in England for his military service, had provided the money for the real indiscreet journey into France,[15] and conversations with him through the spring and summer of 1915 stirred the recollections embodied in "Autumns" I and II, later entitled "The Apple Tree" and "The Wind Blows" and published in the October issues of *Signature*.

This publication, a short-lived fiasco, was intended by Lawrence to be the mouthpiece for a group he hoped to lead toward religious and social reform. Disaffection was immediately manifest in the name of the publication, which Murry chose in order to indicate that the contributors took "no responsibility for one another's creeds." Each man composed his philosophy and each "broke off in the middle." Of his own, Murry later wrote, "I confess that I barely understand it. . . ."[16] Meanwhile Miss Mansfield, utterly unsympathetic toward the clamoring verbosity of either man, published three stories, none of them the "little satirical sketches" Lawrence expected.[17]

"The Little Governess," though printed last, was probably written first. In form, it carries a young woman through a day of travel and sight-seeing and is thus akin to "An Indiscreet Journey," but the young woman through whose mind the adventure is experienced is now naïve, romantic, innocently ignorant. Warned by the lady at the employment bureau which sent her abroad, she is wisely fearful at the beginning of her trip. But Miss Mansfield creates from the outset in the reader an ambivalent attitude toward that advice which would have kept the young girl safe. The lady's remarks, as recalled by the little governess, seem exaggerated:

. . . if you get into a compartment for "Ladies Only" in the train you will be far safer than sleeping in a foreign hotel. Don't go out of the carriage; don't walk about the corridors and *be sure* to lock the lavatory door if you go there. . . . It's better to mistrust people at first rather than trust them, and it's safer to suspect people of evil intentions rather than good ones. . . .

Out of these remarks spring the ironies of the story. The reader, amused by the excessive precautions, is also entertained by the girl's fluctuating feelings of security and fear. In her encounter with the porter she is dutifully, ridiculously mistrustful. Following her instructions, she requests a carriage for women only, and in her obedience to these two admonitions begins her downfall. Angered, the porter places a lascivious old man in her compartment. Because he contrasts with the boisterous, flirtatious young men in the next carriage, she departs injudiciously from her instructions and allows the old man to strike up a conversation. Her arrival at her Munich hotel with this old man reasonably arouses the suspicions of a waiter. Though his insult might have warned her, she takes it for insolence; again, in ignorance of tipping conventions, she antagonizes this man who will complete her ruin. The extent of the waiter's alienation is stressed in a sudden change of viewpoint at the end of the story, when he triumphs, with a heartbeat mad enough to recall Ole Underwood.

A deft structure involves the reader in condoning the ignorant girl's failure to take good advice. Moreover, since the menacing waiter and porter are described from her point of view, the reader might even be compelled to sympathize with her on their account. And again, as she gradually comes to think of the old man as "grandfather," the reader may unsuspectingly accord, though his German title and his recollections of travel to Turkey and attar of roses should remind the Mansfield adept of the mockery of Herr Rat in "Frau Fischer." However, it is hard to maintain sympathy with the girl's excessive joy—she calls this Munich excursion the "happiest day of my life." Her limitations are revealed in her language: what she likes is "nice," "wonderful." She has a "grateful baby heart," and there seems to be some indecision of purpose in Miss Mansfield's portrayal of it. Her carelessness in not discovering that her promenade with the old man will make her late for her appointment is hard to condone. Lack of control and uncertainty of intention seem finally manifest in the shift of viewpoint to the waiter. The reader is left wondering whether the story is focused on the evil aggressions of porters and waiters (which Miss Mansfield suffered from when she traveled alone) or on the ironic advantage of taking excessively good advice.

The technique of "The Apple Tree" is not characteristic. It is a straightforward recollection of an incident in the New Zealand childhood, in which there is apparently no effort to fictionize. The first-person narrator is omniscient; instead of carrying on the usual interior monologue or being concerned with defining her own attitudes, she has penetrated into direct analysis of her father and identifies the little brother Bogey with herself. The materialistic, sensitive father, who "still wondered whether in the deepest sense he got his money's worth," is told by an English visitor that the fruit of the tree—"the accidental thing—the thing that no one had been aware of when the hard bargain was driven [which] . . . hadn't in a way been paid for"—is highly valued. The children, threatened with whipping if they touch the fruit, are able to share a little ironic triumph at harvest time. "Perfect," they say, when stingily granted a taste: thus they leave their father to experience for himself "a floury stuff, a hard, faintly bitter skin—a horrible taste of something dry. . . ." The "strange meaning smile" they exchange belies the final paragraph, which suggests that the children lied to protect their father's feelings.[18]

"The Wind Blows," a sketch, is to some extent written in the same manner. For publication in *Bliss*, the first-person narrator was changed to third person, effecting an increase in immediacy. The wind and the depression and excitement it arouses in the adolescent Matilda account for images and unity. There are several shifts in tone: a frightened awakening at the noise of the wind, a mood in which all its effects are destructive and the realities of life (a phone call from the butcher) ugly, and then the contrasting quiet of a piano studio where the feeling that the music teacher is sympathetic causes tears. Despite that peaceful lull, Matilda, alone again in her bedroom with the wind still blowing, is fearful and recalcitrant in her isolation. Relief and understanding reappear when her brother proposes a walk to the esplanade. The girl bids farewell to her reflection in a mirror; at the dock, seeing a ship departing, she imagines they are both on board. Her perspective shifts to a position on the ship with Bogey many years later as she calls upon him to remember and bids the little island good-by.

The final awareness is of the wind. The story appeared on October 18, 1915, eleven days after Leslie Beauchamp was killed in France. Probably the fantasy ending is related to the intense grief Katherine Mansfield felt at this time.

The stories of the little-magazine period are generally more strongly plotted than those of *In a German Pension:* only four of the twelve later stories are episodes as against nine of the twelve in the earlier work. This contrast between the two groups is even more conspicuous in that it differs strongly from Miss Mansfield's later practice. There are only four plots in the fourteen stories of *Bliss;* only one, in the fifteen of *The Garden-Party.*

The stories of this little-magazine period rarely take comic form and less than half are caustic. The narrators are almost evenly divided between first- and third-person participants in the action, with shifting viewpoints in two stories. They are more sympathetic than the prejudiced girl of *In a German Pension,* and there is a beginning of change in attitude during their stories. Miss Mansfield is nearing the discovery of the value of a fallible narrator, a technique used so far only to characterize Andreas Binzer. This change in the narrator's capacities is a necessary technical reflection of increasing depth of awareness in the writer. In the surprising turns of "Bains Turcs" and "Millie," still akin in pattern to the Chekhovian joke style of the *Pension,* comes revelation of the complexity of human motives. But the advances of the magazine pieces are slight. The greatest value of the experience is probably that it kept the writer at work in the exploration of her craft.

CHAPTER 4

"The Turning Point"

I

J. M. MURRY has described as effecting the turning point in Katherine Mansfield's career the experience of renewed relationship with her brother Leslie and then the shock of his death:

The crucial moment was when, in 1915, her dearly loved younger brother arrived in England to serve as an officer. Her meeting with him formed, as it were, a point around which her changed attitude [a turn to childhood memories, "uncontaminated by the mechanical civilization which had produced the war"] could crystalize. . . . [she] resolved to dedicate herself to recreating life as she had lived and felt it in New Zealand.[1]

Conversations with Leslie were, of course, the immediate impulse which initiated "The Apple Tree," "The Wind Blows," and finally "Prelude." But treatments of New Zealand memories were not unusual for Miss Mansfield. In her first *New Age* period "A Birthday" and "The Breidenbach Family in England" present her family, thinly disguised with German names. Four of her *Rhythm* stories have a New Zealand setting, as does "Millie" for the *Blue Review*. The subject matter of her work, early and late, rises almost entirely from her experience: the New Zealand girlhood, the bohemian world of literary London, the Continental world in which she so frequently convalesced, and occasionally her dreams. Of the fourteen stories in *Bliss*, two recall New Zealand; of the fifteen in *The Garden-Party*, six do so. It never dominates as a source of material, despite the intention expressed in the journal entry of January 22, 1916, "to write about my own country till I simply exhaust my store." [2]

This same entry has been taken as evidence of a sharp change in the form and manner of her stories.[3] She wrote, at the moment,

. . . the form that I would choose has changed utterly. I feel no longer concerned with the same appearance of things. The people who lived or whom I wished to bring into my stories don't interest me any more. The plots of my stories leave me perfectly cold. Granted that these people exist and all the differences, complexities and resolutions are true to them—why should *I* write about them? They are not near me. All the false threads that bound me to them are cut away quite.[4]

But this disavowal cannot be read as defining Miss Mansfield's literary course. It expresses her enthusiasm as she is at work on an early draft of "Prelude." Two years later, in a letter of February 14, 1918, she felt similarly about "Je ne Parle pas Français": "Trouble is I feel I have found an *approach* to a story now which I must apply to everything. Is that nonsense? I read what I wrote before that . . . and I feel: No, this is all *once removed:* It won't do. And it won't. I've got to reconstruct everything." [5] And while she is not completely right in either case—no writer is likely to appraise himself accurately when in the process of composition— a more conspicuous technical innovation is marked by "Je ne Parle pas" than by "Prelude."

In both stories Miss Mansfield was discovering a more dramatic and a more lyric form. Her subjective outlook carried her to a more intense mode of lyricism than that of her avowed master Chekhov. Where Chekhov narrates generalities, Miss Mansfield dramatizes particulars. Where he describes typical family life in a typical provincial town, she portrays a specific family in a precisely detailed location. Chekhov deals with Russia and humanity; Miss Mansfield writes of her own life and her immediate emotional response to it. The result in "Prelude" is a short story much altered from the Chekhovian form she so admired.

To increase dramatic as opposed to narrative quality Miss Mansfield had frequently experimented with detaching herself, the author, from the story. In the early stories this objectivity had been achieved largely by including a first-person narrator who participated in the action. Two variations had moved the stories toward more dramatic form. The first-person narrator is fallible in "Pension Séguin," and several stories are told largely from the viewpoint of a third-person participant. The most successful in this mode before "Something Childish" are the very early "Tiredness of Rosabel" (the omniscient narrator interprets at the end),

"A Birthday" (there is a brief shift to the viewpoint of the servant girl, suggesting an omniscient narrator), "Ole Underwood," "The Little Girl," and "Millie." [6] "The Little Governess," written at about the same time as "The Aloe," employs a third-person, fallible narrator—a device that is technically the greatest advance toward dramatic method. In most of these attempts, however, the diction fails to maintain the limitations which should be imposed by the character of the fictional narrator.

In order to reflect the action of "Prelude" through many minds, Miss Mansfield returns to an omniscient perspective. The vantage point is used to adopt a number of viewpoints; there is no intrusion, no comment by the author. The larger excisions from the original version, "The Aloe," are to eliminate data not immediately relevant to the presentness in time of the story. The backgrounds of the Samuel Josephs family or of Linda Burnell's girlhood serve no purpose in the work as finally conceived. Though known to an omniscient author, they have no place in the consciousness to which that author has limited herself. Thus the final story seems to flow only through the minds of those present as the immediate action elicits their perception. And all of these minds expose themselves, like a cluster of infallible narrators, telling the story from what Erich Auerbach has called a "multipersonal viewpoint." [7]

In this type of shift from mind to mind, with the author apparently eliminated, Miss Mansfield continues until time, too, is controlled by her mentalities—as in the free fluctuations of "The Daughters of the Late Colonel." She discovered the maximum value of the single fallible viewpoint, which controls her second major type of story, in "Je ne Parle pas Français."

No matter what his abstract studies in technique may tell him, discovery for the artist lies ultimately in his own performance. The approach Katherine Mansfield hailed with so much excitement after she wrote "Je ne Parle pas Français" was merely an increase in the fallibility and the distancing of the narrator. For the first time, she portrayed a narrator for whom she felt no sympathy but distinct distaste. That Raoul Duquette tells of the abandoning of the gentle, frightened, courageous Mouse increases the horror of her position and the reader's contempt for him. The very form of the story serves to surround Mouse with depravity.

Before this story could be written and while "The Aloe" was being reworked into "Prelude," Miss Mansfield wrote at least eight pieces for the *New Age*. One appeared November 4, 1915; the others in May, June, September, and October, 1917. Of these, one was a translation from Daudet; three were published in *Bliss;* and one, "The Common Round," was rewritten as "Pictures" for the same volume. The others, more or less like little plays, are of interest as transitional experiments in dramatic form. "Late at Night" is pure monologue; "Stay-Laces" and "Two Tuppenny Ones, Please," monologues with stage directions for silent but excited responses of the speaker's companion; "The Black Cap," dialogues shifting through five scenes. "In Confidence" and "A Picnic" confusedly combine short story and play techniques. In the need of the last three to break through the limitations of dialogue and stage directions, and in the relative freedom of monologue, Miss Mansfield probably found her way to the interior monologue of "Mr. Reginald Peacock's Day," in which the omniscient author is almost entirely effaced. The self-conscious artificialities of Peacock's character also point the way to "Je ne Parle pas Français."

Two more stories may have been written after "Prelude" was completed. "Feuille d'Album" also foreshadows "Je ne Parle pas" by opening the account of a sensitive young man from the distanced viewpoint of a superficial woman, who seems to be telling the story. When she is interrupted by a question from an auditor, the viewpoint becomes multiple through such transitions as "Someone else decided that he ought to fall in love" and " 'What the poor boy really wants is thoroughly rousing,' said a third." The omniscient author intrudes, removing the narrative from "those tender women," and then melts into the viewpoint of the central character himself. The shifts are managed with an ease that is also manifest in "Prelude."

The last and most successful of the *New Age* group, "A Dill Pickle," is contained in the mind of Vera until the end, when she has left the scene and the author must finish. From the conversational recollections of the man and woman who meet by chance after a separation of six years and from her interior monologue the reader infers Vera's lonely need for, yet dissatisfaction with, this man. Though the reader may conclude that her criteria were in some points superficial, after she goes the man's actions confirm her impressions of his parsimony and insensitivity:

> She had gone. He sat there, thunder-struck, astounded beyond words. . . . [Miss Mansfield's dots] And then he asked the waitress for his bill.
> "But the cream has not been touched," he said. "Please do not charge me for it."

This closing with an omniscient viewpoint has almost resulted in the double plotted effect which emerges in "Je ne Parle pas," for it thus completes an implicit story of the past as well as the immediate account of the present.

Mingled with this context of technical experiment was a clarification of attitude. For the *New Age* the stories were necessarily caustic, but upon "Prelude," as upon "Something Childish" and "An Indiscreet Journey," no editorial policy was imposed. Still the satire was not artificial. Miss Mansfield was fastidious. She could be offended by black caps or stinginess, and superficial, selfish responses to the war continued to dishearten her when she became a literary critic for the *Athenaeum*.[8] There was a link between the bitter mockery and the flashes of compassion, which now grew from the sudden insight of "Bains Turcs" to the extended expression of understanding that is "Prelude." During the writing of "Je ne Parle pas," in a letter of February 3, 1918, Miss Mansfield defined the impulses which more or less classify her writing:

> I've two "kick offs" in the writing game. *One* is joy—real joy—the thing that made me write when we lived at Pauline [she worked on "The Aloe" there]. . . . Then something delicate and lovely seems to open before my eyes, like a flower without thought of a frost or a cold breath—knowing that all about it is warm and tender and "ready." And *that* I try, ever so humbly, to express.
> The other "kick off" is my old original one, and, had I not known love, it would have been my all. Not hate or destruction . . . but an *extremely* deep sense of hopelessness, of everything doomed to disaster, almost wilfully, stupidly, like the almond tree and "pas de nougat pour le noel." . . . *a cry against corruption.* . . .[9]

In "Something Childish" and in "An Indiscreet Journey" she had learned through a studied flow of image and paradoxical observation to render implicit in an apparently simple story a complex statement. Each story, in different ways, combined the attitudes Katherine Mansfield described as separate, for each is a cry against the failure or destruction of joy. The failure of young love and the irrational destiny of the forlorn yet comic soldier who sometimes looks like a saint are corruptions to be lamented like the withering of the almond blossom—changes from goodness, beauty, and joy to some lesser state, a falling off, a decay, evil. "Prelude," though she asserts that she tried there to express joy, is everywhere fraught with negative awareness.

II

The title of "Prelude" in its first version, "The Aloe," draws attention instructively to the dominant image of the story. The child Kezia, exploring the grounds of her new home, wanders away from a "tangle of tall dark trees and strange bushes" on "the frightening side, and no garden at all" to the other side of the drive, where she finds a "deeper and deeper tangle of flowers."

In bloom are camellias, syringa, many varieties of roses, fairy bells, geraniums, verbena, lavender, pelagoniums, mignonette, pansies, daisies, red-hot pokers, and sunflowers. The enumeration conveys her pleasure. But, as she turns toward the house, she sees an unknown plant, symbolically located on the "island" which divided the drive into its two arms of opposing character: "Nothing grew on the top [of the island] except one huge plant with thick, grey-green, thorny leaves, and out of the middle there sprang up a tall stout stem. Some of the leaves of the plant were so old that they curled up in the air no longer; they turned back, they were split and broken; some of them lay flat and withered on the ground."

Significantly cut from "Prelude" is the only affirmative sentence in the description. "The Aloe" reads at this point: "but the fresh leaves curled up into the air with their spiked edges; some of them looked as though they had been painted with broad bands of yellow." [10] Nothing fresh or bright remains in the final version. As Linda Burnell, in answer to her daughter Kezia's question, looks at the plant, she sees "its cruel leaves and fleshy stem. High above them, as though becalmed in the air, and yet holding so fast to the earth it grew from, it might have had claws instead of roots. The curving leaves seemed to be hiding something; the blind stem cut into the air as if no wind could ever shake it."

And Kezia learns that it flowers rarely: "Once every hundred years." This is the only moment of kinship between the remote mother and her daughter, as they both sense the menace of the plant. Neither knows the likeness of the other's awareness, yet it is as though each sees here the image of her secret fear: "IT" waiting for Kezia in the silent empty house they have just moved from, "THEY" filling Linda's rooms with threatening anticipation, smiling "their sly secret smile." [11]

In the evening Linda's mother, Mrs. Fairfield, the affirmative and ordering force of the family, discovers buds on the aloe. Linda agrees that the plant is in bud and tells her mother, "I like that aloe. I like it more than anything here. And I am sure I shall remember it long after I've forgotten all the other things." She has envisioned the aloe as a ship, and herself being quickly rowed away upon it, a "more real . . . dream . . . than that they should go back to the house where the sleeping children lay and where Stanley [Linda's husband] and Beryl [her sister] played cribbage." The aloe serves here to reinforce the recurrent motif of Linda's desire to escape. Her morning vision had shown her "driving away from them all in a little buggy, driving away from everybody and not even waving," very much the way she had left Kezia and Lottie, "cast them off," the day before. Again Miss Mansfield increases the negative weight of the symbol, by removing in her final draft all association of Mrs. Fairfield with that flight.[12]

As Linda looks at the aloe, metaphorically the flowering occurs, but it is a flowering of realization in her own mind: "From below she could see the long sharp thorns that edged the aloe leaves, and at the sight of them her heart grew hard. . . . [Miss Mansfield's dots] She particularly liked the long sharp thorns. . . . Nobody would dare to come near the ship or to follow after." As her mind follows the train of thought unleashed by her response to the aloe, she recognizes her hatred, despite "all her love and respect and admiration," of Stanley: "It had never been so plain to her as it was at this moment. There were all her feelings for him, sharp and defined, one as true as the other. And there was this other, this hatred, just as real as the rest."

As she came to this knowledge, yielding to the destructive violence of the aloe, she "snatched her hand from mother's arm." Her gesture underlines the story's polarities: serenity, goodness, order, manifest in every action and word of Mrs. Fairfield, and the ominous menace implicit in the silent, unmoving appearance of the aloe. Between their rival claims waver Linda and Kezia, the major characters of the story. Linda concludes negatively, finding life absurd, her desire to live a mania, and the future promising more of what she has, more of what she does not want: children, money, and gardens, "with whole fleets of aloes in them." The menace will intensify.

With Kezia the conclusion is less clear, for Kezia's consciousness is less mature, less fixed than her mother's. The two are parallel not only in their fears and in their feeling for the aloe, but, of course, in their need for Mrs. Fairfield, the only answer to that menace. Linda clearly recognizes that order is the adjunct of her mother. Finding her in the kitchen where under her hand "everything . . . had become part of a series of patterns," Linda comments: "It says 'mother' all over; everything is in pairs." And watching her, Linda is aware of her own need: "There was something comforting in the sight of her that Linda felt she could never do without. She needed the sweet smell of her flesh, and the soft feel of her cheeks and her arms and shoulders still softer." But waking that morning, Linda had seen the orderliness of the bedroom, in which "all the furniture had found a place—all the old paraphernalia—" and she had rejected it. "Looking at them she wished that she was going away from this house, too."

Kezia is too young to think about her relationship to her grandmother, but in the two days of "Prelude" she turns often to the comfort of this orderly woman. It is the grandmother she wishes to kiss good-by, when she and little sister Lottie are left behind with the unmoved furniture. Characteristically, in this scene, the grandmother has settled on the plan of leaving the children with Mrs. Samuel Josephs while Linda only associates them whimsically with the tables and chairs standing on their heads on the front lawn. How absurd they looked! Either they ought to be the other way up, or Lottie and Kezia ought to stand on their heads, too. And she longed to say, "Stand on your heads, children, and wait for the storeman." It seemed to her that would be so exquisitely funny that she could not attend to Mrs. Samuel Josephs.

From "How absurd. . . ." this passage was added in revision, clearly to emphasize Linda's irresponsibility and to anticipate her final view of life.

Kezia explores disorder but usually turns away from it. She pokes in the rubbish left in her family's old house and knows there will be none left in her grandmother's room. She wanders away from or resists the games devised by her older sister, but even in her recalcitrance (surely she is the "lady-help" who carelessly says, "Oh, well, it doesn't matter," when Isabel wonders whether a maid should be introduced to a caller) she behaves with the orderly habit of Mrs. Fairfield:

She began to lay the cloth on a pink garden seat. In front of each person she put two geranium leaf plates, a pine needle fork and a twig knife. There were three daisy heads on a laurel leaf for poached eggs, some slices of fuchia petal cold beef, some lovely little rissoles made of earth and water and dandelion seeds, and the chocolate custard which she decided to serve in the pawa shell she had cooked it in.

These miniature and imaginative precisions are akin to the match-box surprise she plans to make for her grandmother.

Sometimes disorder discomfits her. The empty house grew frightening. She looked at the bull which Linda airily thought had tossed her, but she "had not liked the bull frightfully, so she had walked away. . . ." In the garden, she turned from the dark side of strange bushes where the paths were ill-kept to the side where the paths had box edges and the flowers were known. Amid this pleasant beauty she thought of her grandmother.

For Kezia the most intense conflict of order with the menace occurs in the beheading of the duck: "[Pat] put down the body and it began to waddle—with only a long spurt of blood where the head had been; it began to pad away without a sound towards the steep bank that led to the stream. . . . [Miss Mansfield's dots] That was the crowning wonder."

Even in death the nervous system mysteriously attempts the patterned behavior of life. At that Kezia cries out for the restoration of order: "Put head back! Put head back!" For a moment she is violent in her grief. Then, like her mother, she finds a consolation in some immediacy: the strangeness of Pat's gold earrings. Linda will turn from her rejection of life, brought on by the sight of the cruel aloe, to the scent of verbena, the beauty of camellia trees, and her mother's companionship.

But if there is a direction in the author's attitude it is negative. The duck's head cannot be put back. Linda does, despite her love, hate Stanley, fear childbearing, prefer the aloe. Order to her mother involves an acceptance of life—its work, its pain, its Stanleys. Mrs. Fairfield can make it all into something of calm beauty, but this order, Linda feels, is killing her; from the productive life of Stanley and her mother she flees, in her indifference, to aloofness, even to mockery of their realities: food, economy, well-arranged kitchens, children, sexual relations. She would like to run away in fact as well as in imagination.

The last word is not Mrs. Fairfield's, as, unaware of Linda's vision of the aloe, she thinks of turning the fruit into jam. Final emphasis lies in the implications of the last scene, that between Beryl and Kezia. Throughout much of the story Beryl has helped with the moving, "slaved" toward the creation of order in the house. But her work has not been like the creative work of her mother. Beryl is sullen, resents the move to the country, is negative in her treatment of the children. She deplores Stanley's taste and his demands; yet, because the pose pleases her, probably as a contrast to her indifferent older sister, she flirts with him over the cribbage board. In the final scene, in which she is writing a letter, she becomes disgusted with herself and reviews her behavior:

"Oh," she cried, "I am so miserable—so frightfully miserable. I know that I am silly and spiteful and vain; I'm always acting a part. I'm never my real self for a moment."

. . . .
If she had been happy and leading her own life, her false life would cease to be. She saw the real Beryl—a shadow . . . a shadow. Faint

and unsubstantial she shone. What was there of her except the radiance? And for what tiny moments she was really she. . . . At those
times she had felt: "Life is rich and mysterious and good, and I am
rich and mysterious and good, too." Shall I ever be that Beryl for ever?
Shall I? How can I? And was there ever a time when I did not have
a false self?

This is Beryl's cry against corruption, and the answer seems to
appear in Kezia's entrance. Kezia brings a call to lunch and the
news that father has brought a man home. She carries a "very
dirty calico cat." When Beryl has gone, Kezia meddles with things
not her own. She sets the top of Beryl's cream jar upon the cat's
ear. The cat falls and with it the cream jar lid.

[It] flew through the air and rolled like a penny in a round on the
linoleum—and did not break.
But for Kezia it had broken the moment it flew through the air, and
she picked it up, hot all over, and put it back on the dressing table.
Then she tip-toed away, far too quickly and airily. . . . [Miss Mansfield's dots]

So Kezia, too, is a pretender and, for the moment, false. Thus she
answers Beryl's question: "And was there ever a time when I did
not have a false self?"
Ending here, "Prelude" appears to portray four stages of
womanhood. Kezia, the child, reaches for the order and serenity
of her grandmother, who draws strength from her committal to
practical reality. The adolescent Beryl would like to be real but
finds herself almost entirely false. Her romantic dreams of court-
ship by a lover with money contrast with Linda's appraisal as a
woman who has secured love, marriage, and security, but finds
realistic disadvantages in these objectives. For Kezia and Beryl,
the two days of the story describe a prelude, a beginning, but for
Linda the game is apparently up. Her rejection is made even more
conclusive in that she, unlike Beryl, knows her mother's worth.
Perhaps Beryl and Kezia can attain the affirmative state of Mrs.
Fairfield. But Kezia's easy distraction from her protest at the
duck's death, her final stealthy posture, the predominant falsity of
Beryl, and, above all, the crucial significance of the aloe leave the

final emphasis on the passing of innocence and on the victory, in the withering blossom, of corruption.

" 'What form it is?' you ask," Miss Mansfield wrote to Dorothy Brett, the October after she had finished the revision. "Ah, Brett, it's so difficult to say. As far as I know, it's more or less my own invention." [13] The innovation lies in letting the story unfold in the immediacy of many consciousnesses, rendered by the self-effacing projection of the omniscient author. Interpretation of the sort continually imposed upon nearly every act of his characters by the all-knowing, distant Chekhov is avoided. The reader learns the thoughts and feelings of the characters only from their own responses. No characterization is adulterated by dependence upon another. The reader, as with a Chekhov story, is left to infer the final meaning; however, Miss Mansfield compels her reader to work more immediately upon the data. As in a poem, she holds him poised upon the turns of each mind, so that he moves in the experiences, and creates himself the larger complex, the characters' and his own interwoven responses, which, for the careful reader, will be something near that experience toward which the author's control has led him. This involvement of the reader in multiple viewpoints, so easily overlapped that it is sometimes difficult in the later stories to specify when the change occurred, is Katherine Mansfield's most influential contribution to the modern short story.

III

In the early months of 1916 at Bandol, while Miss Mansfield was at work on "The Aloe," Murry wrote his first book of literary criticism, *Fyodor Dostoyevsky.* Miss Mansfield's *Journal* and *Scrapbook*[14] indicate, as would be expected, that she took an interest in the study. When she sent Murry the first part of "Je ne Parle pas Français," he wrote excitedly, ". . . my sensation is like that which I had when I read Dostoyevsky's *Letters from the Underworld.* . . . It's utterly unlike any sensation I have ever yet had from any writing of yours, or any writing at all except Dostoyevsky's." [15] She herself could only exclaim, "I read the fair copy just now and couldn't think where the devil I had got the bloody thing from—I can't even now." [16] But, in the broadest outline, the story does have a kinship in tone, characterization, and form to Dostoyevsky's short novel. In the Russian work an egotistical man, part sadist, part masochist, with literary pretensions, reveals in first person his own loathsome nature. Within the account of his life he includes, because the snow is falling, a rather lengthy story called "A propos of the Wet Snow." This recollection of an earlier experience in his life occupies two thirds of the novel, which ends immediately upon the end of the anecdote.

The shape of "Je ne Parle pas" is similar, but it has been concentrated in a short story. A greater change is that Raoul Duquette, the encompassing narrator, by acting as a narrator on the fringe of one story, paradoxically tells two other stories of himself. The crisis of the first is the failure of Dick Harmon to remain in France with Mouse after their elopement. Raoul Duquette's echoic rejection only confirms his exposé of his character and provides him with a point of departure for the tale of his "grand moment." That he encircles it with a third story, an apparently irrelevant account of himself, conveys simultaneously his sterile effeminacy and his overweening self-esteem. To him the point of major significance is not that Mouse has been left desolate in Paris, but that he, who abandoned her after knowing fully her helplessness, can at the recollection experience "such an intensity of feeling so . . . [Miss Mansfield's dots] purely." However, this view, his mannered style, and the arrangement of materials are calculated more importantly to damn him than to lament the fate of Mouse. The form of the story serves to engulf Mouse in the horror that is the narrator's character.

The arrangement of the encircling story is deceptively simple; it is based on the raising of curiosity in the reader and then, after a small delay in which character and setting are exposed, satisfying that curiosity. "I do not know why I have such a fancy for this little café"—the opening sentence—calls for a description of the "dirty and sad, sad" place and its clientele, with a "long and rather far-fetched digression" in which the reader is told that Duquette does not believe in the human soul, and infers from his style that he is artificial and self-conscious. The key passage is slyly buried in the digression, when the narrator images himself as a customs official examining the portmanteaux, his metaphor for people, "packed with certain things. . . ." "Have you anything to declare?" he asks: "And the moment of hesitation as to whether I am going to be fooled just before I chalk that squiggle, and then the other moment of hesitation just after, as to whether I have been, are perhaps the two most thrilling instants in life. Yes, they are, to me." This describes his position with regard to Dick and Mouse— his avid, dehumanized interest in their feelings as they act out their failure.

After this much exposition the reader learns that Duquette likes the café because he experienced there a moment of intense feeling. There is another delay, rich with self-exposure, as the preparation for the moment is described; then he notices on a blotting paper seized to record a "rather nice . . . bit about the Virgin," "that stupid, stale little phrase: *Je ne parle pas français.*" At which the moment occurs:

> How can I describe it? I didn't think of anything. I didn't even cry out to myself. Just for one moment I was not. I was Agony, Agony, Agony.
> Then it passed, and the very second after I was thinking: "Good God! Am I capable of feeling as strongly as that?
> . . . .
> And up I puffed and puffed, blowing off finally with: "After all I must be first-rate. No second-rate mind could have experienced such an intensity of feeling so . . . purely."

As the reader wonders about the cause of the moment, he learns that Duquette has "made it a rule of [his] life never to regret and never to look back," but even as he writes this, his "other self has been chasing up and down out in the dark there," looking unsuccessfully "like a lost dog" for a girl named Mouse. With that much of a promise to lure him, the reader is led through several more pages of Duquette autobiography and finally to the story of the attempted elopement of Mouse and Dick. The high-flown description of his "moment" early in the story, followed by the steady exposure of his composed enjoyment of suffering, results in a deterioration of the reader's opinion; in the end the narrator says, "Of course, you know what to expect." So at last the cause of the moment is known. He abandoned Mouse, but he does remember her. And that is the story of his banality, by which ironically he sets out to demonstrate that he is "first-rate."

That his proof rests upon his response to the phrase which most

completely expressed Mouse's helplessness in Paris is the peak of
his insensitivity. Her last words to Duquette, as she accepted his
offer of help, were "It makes things rather difficult because . . .
je ne parle pas français." And Duquette insistently labors the
effect upon him of that remark. Having exposed his callousness,
his perverted childhood, and his career as gigolo, and imaged
himself as a dog and a woman, he reveals that this event is his
only compensation for a latent lack of self-respect:

> If you think what I've written is merely superficial and impudent and
> cheap you're wrong. I'll admit it does sound so, but then it is not at all.
> If it were, how could I have experienced what I did when I read that
> stale little phrase written in green ink, in the writing-pad? That proves
> there's more in me and that I really am important, doesn't it? Anything
> a fraction less than that moment of anguish I might have put on. But
> no! That was real!

Besides the implication of his failure to act and the many details
of his own self-description, the motif of a song runs through the
story to provide a further comment. It is Dick's English song
about a homeless man looking for dinner. The time of two of the
stories Duquette tells—the enveloping story and the story of the
moment—is afternoon. In each the occasion for entering the café
is that he "was drifting along, either going home or not going
home." The wide variety of his experiences with women has been
stated, and that they always have "made the first advances." The
proprietress of the café he favors is described as restless, as hope-
lessly pretending to look for someone she knows will not come.
The story ends:

> I must go. I must go. I reach down my coat and hat. Madame knows
> me. "You haven't dined yet?" she smiles.
> "No, not yet, Madame."

There is an implication here that this hungry, hollow man, who
has fed so avidly on the sorrows of Mouse and of Dick Harmon,
will continue his parasitic ventures in another meal, feasting this
time on the less moving loneliness of Madame.[17]
The form of this story was very important to Katherine Mansfield. "I've got to reconstruct everything," was her first appraisal.

She never repeated it quite so elaborately. "A Married Man's Story," according to Murry's note, begun in May when she wrote, "I have started working—another member of the *Je ne Parle pas* family, I fondly dream—" [18] is similar in shape, but it was not finished. The only finished story close in form is "Poison," a much briefer incident enclosing the narrator's story of a youthful experience in his own older viewpoint.

The intricacy of structure of "Je ne Parle pas Français" did not matter so much as the utter removal of author, the very full realization of character and scene solely through a single point of view, and the free shifts in time made possible through that limitation. Beginning with "Bliss," many of the stories told from the viewpoint of a third person narrator take on, with an increase in subtlety, this aspect of the form of "Je ne Parle pas." Others continue the multipersonal discoveries of "Prelude," with an effaced omniscient author moving among several points of view. In either case, time is dealt with very freely through the exploitation of interior monologue, and meaning remains implicit in a paradoxical interplay of gesture, thought, and image.

Now the craft was found, and the depths of the consciousness so deeply plumbed that Murry, in his letter about "Je ne Parle pas," declared such a practice dangerous. Five years remained for the artist to convey her vision. She had discovered its substance and the method. Her conviction and passion are evident in a letter of November 16, 1919:

Now [after the war] we know ourselves for what we are. In a way it's a tragic knowledge: it's as though, even while we live again, we face death. But *through Life:* that's the point. We see death in life as we see death in a flower that is fresh unfolded. Our hymn is to the flower's beauty: we would make that beauty immortal because we *know.*

. . . .

I mean "deserts of vast eternity." But . . . I couldn't tell anybody *bang out* about those deserts: they are my secret. I might write about a boy eating strawberries or a woman combing her hair on a windy morning, and that is the only way I can ever mention them. But they *must* be there. Nothing less will do.[19]

She would write out to the end her perceptions of beauty and her cry against its corruption.

CHAPTER 5

Trains of Thought

I

"J E NE PARLE PAS" was scarcely finished when Miss Mansfield dreamed and immediately wrote the short story "Sun
and Moon." "It was very light," [1] she wrote Murry, but the cry
against corruption was nonetheless there. When five-year-old Sun
sees the little ice-cream house "broken—broken and half melted
away," the offer of sweets does not appease him. He wails loudly
and declares this passing of prettiness "horrid." Within two weeks
of the composition, Miss Mansfield was beginning to disavow it.
"Would the *Nation* publish *Sun and Moon?*" she asked Murry. "If
they publish that rubbish by ——— I think they might." [2] Nearly
two years later: "No, Boge [pet name for Murry], don't send A.
and L. [*Arts and Letters*] *Sun and Moon,* if you don't mind. (1)
They'd not publish it (2) I feel far away from it." And on September 17, 1920: "Even though I'm poor as a Mouse don't publish *Sun
and Moon.*" [3] But Murry, then editor of the *Athenaeum,* probably
had it in print by then, for the story appeared on October 1.

Miss Mansfield had written stories about children throughout
her career, always with singular insight into their psychology. Perhaps because the material came easily as the result of dreams or
of a capacity for total recall, she did not seem to value them
highly. "My serious stories won't ever bring me anything but my
'child' stories ought to and my light ones, once I find a place," she
told Murry in February, 1918. [4] She could not know then that she
would write only three more "'child' stories": "See-Saw," scarcely
a sketch, the trivial "Sixpence," and the very wonderful "A Doll's
House" which plumbs the depths of the New Zealand vein.

II

At the other extreme were her satirical views of the pseudo-
artistic life of artists and the hangers-on of artistic life. This, indeed, was the world she could endure no more easily than she had

submitted to the world of the German *pension*. But her pen had grown subtler. Moving through a few hours of a day or, at the most, a week-end, she let these people expose themselves. In the dialogue or interior monologues of "Psychology," "Revelations," and "A Dill Pickle" she needed only a brief encounter to delineate shallowness.

In "Mr. Reginald Peacock's Day" it took just that long. The consciousness of this affected singing teacher reveals a man hypersensitive to his own comfort. His many female students and the idle, wealthy women who hear his concerts gush adulation. But his wife only manages the household and their young son for his convenience. Though he does not acknowledge it, his petulant selfishness has deprived her of the servant he rebukes her for not having. Throughout the day, as he teaches and dines with affable ladies, he repeats to any advance, "Dear lady, I should be only too charmed." At the end of his very successful day, moved by the condescension and champagne of a noble lord, he would like to tell his wife of his triumphs, ". . . try to treat her as a friend, to tell her everything, to win her." But he is trapped by his own artificiality and can utter only the empty phrase he reserves for the other ladies. The ironic summation of his behavior is found in an adoring lady's letter—"You are teaching the world to escape from life."

Rosemary Fell, the smart, affluent, but insincere young woman of "A Cup of Tea," damns herself, like Raoul Duquette, through avidity for an exciting experience which feeds on another's misery. The story is viewed by an omniscient narrator who stylistically adopts a persona very close to that of Rosemary herself. The voice of the opening paragraph is malicious:

Rosemary Fell was not exactly beautiful. No, you couldn't have called her beautiful. Pretty? Well, if you took her to pieces . . . But why be so cruel as to take anyone to pieces? She was young, brilliant, extremely modern . . . and her parties were the most delicious mixture of the really important people and . . . artists—quaint creatures, discoveries of hers, some of them too terrifying for words, but others quite presentable and amusing. [Miss Mansfield's dots]

When the narrator moves to a reflection of Rosemary's thinking, it is hard to tell the difference. Meeting the hungry girl on the street,

Rosemary thinks, "It was like something out of a novel by Dostoyevsky, this meeting in the dusk. Supposing she took the girl home? Supposing she did do one of those things she was always reading about or seeing on the stage, what would happen? It would be thrilling. And she heard herself saying afterward to the amazement of her friends. . . ."

Rosemary is artificial, idle, insensitive. The contrast between the five pounds she reduces to three as a gift to the penniless girl and the useless but pretty twenty-eight-guinea box she asks of her husband reveals her selfish materialism. But the final detail of her exposure dwells on her insecure vanity, the real reason for dismissing the young woman whom her husband called "astonishingly pretty . . . absolutely lovely." The words echo in Rosemary's mind as she finds money for the girl. Later she has "just done her hair, darkened her eyes a little, and put on her pearls," when she whispers to her husband, "Philip . . . am I pretty?"

The malicious arrangement of data is augmented by the malicious tone of the narrator. It is as though such behavior deserves no compassion. The fallibility of the narrator's mood motivates the organization but does not call into question the facts of the case. The conception of the story has altered considerably from "The Dark Hollow," [5] a first study of similar relations between two women. In this early and unfinished draft the two are old schoolmates. The penniless one, however, instead of merely weeping, tells a false story of her hard life to the kind, generous friend who has determined to take her in. The shift of the needy girl to a lower social position may have controlled Miss Mansfield's sympathy.[6] Though she often complained in her letters of the crudity and incompetence of servants and of other "inferiors," this illiberal sentiment she apparently feared might be snobbery. The final literary statements were always compassionate.

In "Marriage à la Mode" and in "Bliss" Miss Mansfield moved to the condemnation of groups. Murry has described these stories as "semi-sophisticated" failures. He feels that "the stupider *intelligentsia*" is the subject and that "the discordant combination of caricature with emotional pathos . . . spoils" them both.[7] But these discords in "Marriage . . ." intensify the sense of William's puzzled, honest anguish when he is confronted by the falseness of Isabel and her crowd. In "Bliss" the fact that Bertha in her excited anticipation must await her climax and then see it turn to dust is well accompanied by the sterility of her guests. As doubtful as Murry's are Miss Berkman's criticisms that "William's unhappy soliloquies . . . are scarcely masculine" and that Bertha's "overwrought, gushing manner . . . alienates sympathy. . . ." [8] However, the intention of these effects deserves further examination.

When Miss Mansfield chooses to portray an effeminate man, she selects for him a characterizing diction and syntax. Raoul Duquette, Reginald Peacock, Bobby Kane of "Marriage à la Mode," and Eddie Warren of "Bliss" are all excessively articulate. "Charming" is not only the echoic word of Peacock, but it frequently runs through the mind of Duquette. Eddie Warren describes too many experiences as *dreadful,* and italics indicate that the rhythms of his speech are those of a gushing woman. His exaggerated descriptions—"so wonderful," "deeply true"—are paralleled by Duquette's "so exactly the gesture," "so tender, so reassuring," "so amazingly in the picture," and by Bobby Kane's "really look too divine" and "a perfect little ballet." All are conscious of themselves, ranging from delighted admiration of white sox to operatic gestures in the bathtub.

None of these stances are William's. He reads business papers and meditates about the change in Isabel, but the language of his monologue at its most poetic is manly. His farthest flight is a memory of childhood:

The exquisiteness freshness of Isabel! When he had been a little boy, it was his delight to run into the garden after a shower of rain and shake the rose-bush over him. Isabel was that rose-bush, petal-soft, sparkling and cool. And he was still that little boy. But there was no running into the garden now, no laughing and shaking. The dull, persistent gnawing in his breast started again.

His conversation is laconic, inexpressive. Of his love letter there is quoted one straightforward sentence: "God forbid, my darling, that I should be a drag on your happiness." It is just his down-to-earth mien and his resulting inability to play a part among Isabel's pretentious friends that causes his alienation. William is, in fact, a rather neutral figure who wins sympathy only because the group which causes his misery is cruel and tasteless. Greedy, idle, and dull, Isabel and her friends reach a peak of bad taste in their mockery of William's letter. That Isabel—even recognizing that the incident was "vile, odious, abominable, vulgar"—cannot re-form completes the analysis of her character and exposes it as William's greatest disaster.

In "Bliss" Miss Mansfield intentionally portrays Bertha's manner as "overwrought." She is, as Miss Berkman suggests, hysterical and recognizes it herself as she begins to laugh at the end of the first section of the story. Again and again through the evening Bertha controls her rising laughter. Repeatedly it is clear that she is attempting unsuccessfully to deceive herself. Concerning her guests her self-deception is not immediately obvious:

They had people coming to dinner. The Norman Knights—a very sound couple—he was about to start a theatre, and she was awfully keen on interior decoration, a young man, Eddie Warren, who had just published a little book of poems and whom everybody was asking to dine, and a "find" of Bertha's called Pearl Fulton. . . . Bertha had fallen in love with her, as she always did fall in love with beautiful women who had something strange about them.

But, when the guests arrive, Mrs. Knight looks to Bertha "like a very intelligent monkey," and her mind pursues the image, dressing the woman in banana skins, pretending that she hoards nuts in her bodice and that she is cold without her red flannel jacket, typical monkey garb. The silent mockery mounts until "Bertha had to dig her nails into her hands—so as not to laugh too much." Mr. Knight's gestures with his monocle appear equally absurd to her. And conversation with Eddie must also be stifled to avoid rudeness. When he tells her that there is a moon, "She wanted to cry: 'I am sure there is—often—often,'" and later she thinks of "poor Eddie's moon."

It is clear then that what Bertha tells herself and the responses she makes to stimuli within the story are in conflict. This is the key to what otherwise would be a badly controlled story. She is a treacherously fallible narrator. The conflict between deliberately verbalized attitude and attitude conveyed by gesture or unbidden feeling must be examined in order to grasp her dealings with Pearl Fulton and with her husband Harry. It is very likely that her high excitement, which she interprets at first as "bliss" but very shortly calls "hysteria," has arisen because she knows before the story begins that her husband is having an affair with a woman, and perhaps she even senses that the woman may be Pearl Fulton.

The hysterical tone of her monologue is due to her attempt to compensate, to keep from acknowledging consciously what she must deeply suspect. For this reason, she "hardly dared to breathe for fear of fanning . . . higher" the feeling she finds "almost unbearable." And "she hardly dared to look into the cold mirror," but when she does, she declares herself "radiant, with smiling, trembling lips, with big dark eyes, and an air of listening, waiting for something . . . divine to happen . . . that she knew must happen . . . infallibly." [Miss Mansfield's dots] Only two words, *radiant* and *divine*, her judgments of her appearance and feeling, make affirmative a passage ironic with foreboding.

That her judgments cannot be trusted is again evident when she considers her life with Harry. First, there is the significance of the arrangement of events. All is ready for the party. Waiting, Bertha looks out the windows at the pear tree "in fullest, richest bloom; it stood perfect, as though becalmed against the jade-green sky." Immediately she also sees two cats, one creeping after another. This uneasiness before animal sexuality, which becomes clear later when she identically images Eddie's departure with Miss Fulton, deepens to nervous pacing, a stifled feeling: ". . . as though overcome, she flung down on a couch and pressed her hands to her eyes. 'I'm too happy—too happy!' she murmured." At this point she sees the pear tree as a symbol of her life. The compensation for whatever unbidden fears the prowling cats aroused is immediate and intense in the monologue which follows:

Really—really she had everything. She was young. Harry and she were as much in love as ever, and they got on together splendidly, and were really good pals. She had an adorable baby. They didn't have to worry about money. They had this absolutely satisfactory house and garden. And friends—modern, thrilling friends, writers and painters and poets or people keen on social questions—just the kind of friends they wanted. And then there were books and there was music, and she had found a wonderful little dressmaker, and they were going abroad in the summer, and their new cook made the most superb omelettes. . . . [Miss Mansfield's dots]

Bertha cuts herself off quite accurately: "I'm absurd. Absurd!"

Absurd or pathetic, even her style gives her away. "Really—really—" she tries to persuade herself, assembling too many adjectives and adverbs to suggest conviction. "As much in love *as ever*" clashes ironically with "got on . . . splendidly" and "really good pals." The friends she knows too well. Her tapering off into dressmaker and cook after the diversion of the arts admits failure. For, in fact, the environment yields Bertha little satisfaction. She is cut off from both Harry and the baby. She does not "dare" question the nurse's authority nor can she, wanting "to get in touch with [Harry] for a moment," speak to him emotionally over the phone. Even her communication with Miss Fulton is "provoking," for at a certain point Miss Fulton's frankness ceases and Bertha "couldn't yet make her out."

That she cannot express her feelings Bertha blames on "idiotic civilization," asking "Why be given a body if you have to keep it shut up in a case like a rare, rare fiddle?" Feeling a similar absurdity with the nurse, she repeats the image: "Why have a baby if it has to be kept—not in a case like a rare, rare fiddle—but in another woman's arms?" It is like an incremental repetition which could prove circular. The question, implicit at the end of the story, this time beginning "Why have a husband if," may be latent in the nursery scene. For Bertha confronts not only the nurse but Pearl Fulton, too, "like the poor little girl in front of the rich little girl with the doll." This is Bertha's true image of herself; she is impoverished, denied, too absurdly civilized to act. Her frustration lies in her knowledge that, if she is in full bloom like the pear tree, she is also, like it, "becalmed."

What then is the reader, dependent upon Bertha's fallible point of view, to make of her relations with Harry and Pearl Fulton? In a letter of March 14, 1918, Miss Mansfield acknowledged that the newly written story was too subtle: "What I *meant* . . . was Bertha, not being an artist, was yet artist *manquée* enough to realize that these words and expressions were not and couldn't be hers. They were, as it were, *quoted* by her, borrowed with . . . an eyebrow . . . yet she'd none of her own. But this, I agree, is not permissible. I can't grant all that in my dear reader." [Miss Mansfield's dots] [9] No first draft remains to account for these remarks, and quotations remained in the monologues when the revised and presumably clearer version appeared in the August *English Review*. In my judgment, the careful and repeated patterning of compensatory interior monologue is belied by insistent emotional reflexes, gestures, or censored speech which reveal Bertha's unhappy awareness.

Why else has Bertha so compulsively talked to Harry of Miss Fulton, eliciting so many satisfactorily negative comments? How is it that, upon his late arrival home, "she talked and laughed and positively forgot until he had come in . . . that Pearl Fulton had not turned up"? (*Positively* is the stylistic excess that arouses doubt.) Again, as they wait for Miss Fulton to come in from her taxi, why is the group uneasy in Bertha's view? "Came another tiny moment [what other moment is referred to?], while they waited, laughing and talking, just a trifle too much at their ease, a trifle too unaware. And then Miss Fulton . . . came in. . . ." Of what are they "too unaware"? The implication is clearly that Bertha, suspecting some relationship between Miss Fulton and her husband, feels that the guests also know of it.

Immediately upon touching the woman's arm to lead her in to dinner, Bertha starts "blazing—blazing" with what she calls "the fire of bliss." Thus she interprets the feeling she thinks she shares with her rival. Though Miss Fulton does *not* look at her, Bertha insists to herself "as if the longest, most intimate look had passed between them—as if they had said to each other: 'You, too?'—that Pearl Fulton . . . was feeling just what she was feeling." It seems more likely that Bertha, who is acknowledgedly frigid in her sexual relations with Harry, is trying (and has been all day) to persuade herself that she feels "just what" the woman who is loved by her husband does. For Bertha knows that her evening costume of green and white echoes the pear tree, though she tells herself it is unintentional. She has also chosen the colors of the food she knows Harry desires; in her mind she quotes him on his "shameless passion for the white flesh of the lobster" and "the green of pistachio ices—green and cold like the eyelids of Egyptian dancers." But this last and most sensual of his images she cannot imitate. That is left to Miss Fulton with her "heavy eyelids" and her mysterious look. She also achieves a greater appearance of coldness in her silver dress, through which she too partakes of the image of the pear tree in moonlight. The cold and silvery image implicit in the name Pearl reinforces her likeness.[10] Beside Miss Fulton, Bertha is rather puppylike, a "pal" trying to please Harry, who could have wept like a child because he admires the soufflé.

I think Bertha is making a tremendous attempt, as she looks at the pear tree, to share the passion of Pearl Fulton simply because that is her only weapon against the woman. But the very thought of bed, darkness, and Harry terrifies her—no matter what her dubious assertions in her panicked frame of mind. The cruelest irony she inflicts upon herself is her thought that "in bed to-night" she will try to explain to Harry "What she and I have shared." That she senses they have shared Harry is clear, for all unbidden comes the emotional response to the censored thought: "At those last words something strange and almost terrifying darted into Bertha's mind." The passage which follows economically conveys both her suspicion of Harry and her fear of sexual relations, but again she censors her subconscious, imposing upon it the doubtful assertion: "For the first time in her life Bertha Young desired her husband." It is, incidentally, the second and last time in the story that her artfully chosen surname is mentioned. The first time is the beginning: "Although Bertha Young was thirty. . . ." The implication is obvious: Bertha is immature, and in that respect somewhat ridiculous.

But, despite her flaws, Bertha has Miss Mansfield's sympathy. Surely she was thinking of this type of woman when more than two years later she wrote: "These half people are very queer— very tragic, really. They are neither simple—nor are they artists. They are between the two and yet they have the desires (no, appetites) of both." [11] Though Bertha physically rejects Harry, even to seeing him grotesquely as he surreptitiously woos Miss Fulton in the hall, she has most sensitively perceived the beauty of the pear tree. And though Bertha is immature and has falsified herself throughout the story, she instinctively affirms life at the end. Deluded by no pathetic fallacy, she runs to the window in her final, undeniable knowledge and sees "the pear tree was as lovely as ever and as full of flower and as still." The affirmation retains its complexity, however, for the final emphasis is on stillness. The pear tree continues to suggest Bertha and to be itself. If, as Miss Berkman well indicates, the theme of "Bliss" is "the immutability of natural beauty in the face of human disaster," [12] it is also that from the human point of view such beauty offers no promise: it is "becalmed."

But "Bliss" is more than a story in itself. It occupies a mid position in a chain of stories, linking "Something Childish But Very Natural" and "Poison" in Miss Mansfield's developing consideration of the failure of love between men and women. The connection is evident when in "Poison" Beatrice sings, "Had I two little feathery wings/And were a little feathery bird . . ."—two lines, slightly altered, of the poem which gives the earlier story its title. The next line, "To you I'd fly, my dear," had she sung it, would have made explicit the fact mentioned by Miss Mansfield in a letter explaining the story, that "she expects a letter from someone calling her away." [13] But the nameless and adoring young man does not know the poem. "You wouldn't fly away?" he asks, and Beatrice replies that she would fly only to meet the postman, not explaining further that in the expected letter lies her shifting heart.

Miss Mansfield herself has provided a detailed explication of this story. Of interest is her intricate conception of the narrator:

The story is told by (evidently) a worldly, rather cynical (not wholly cynical) man *against* himself (but not altogether) when he was so absurdly young. You know how young by his idea of what woman is. She has been up to now only the *vision*, only she who passes. . . . And he has put *all* his passion into this Beatrice. . . . He, of course, laughs at it now, and laughs at her. . . . But he also regrets the self who, dead privately, would have been young enough to have actually wanted to *Marry* such a woman. . . . And the story is told by the man who gives himself away and hides his traces at the same moment.[14]

The theme, she adds, is "the lament for youthful belief." This phrase describes "Something Childish But Very Natural" as well. In both a young man wants to marry an idolized woman, but in "Poison" the affair has progressed beyond the childish. It is, in Miss Mansfield's words, "promiscuous love." Curiously, in "Poison," written seven years after the first one, the young man is twenty-four, seven years older than Henry of "Something Childish." Like Edna, Beatrice smiles "dreamily," and the menace of her dreaminess is in her immediately expressed desire for mail. Even the feeling of Henry's disillusionment is reproduced through allusive similarities of image. The conclusive telegram is brought to Henry by a little girl whom he sees as a moth. As he looks at it, he thinks it perhaps make-believe, containing a make-believe snake, an idea which ironically foreshadows his poisoning. In "Poison" the postman comes as a blue beetle, and the poison itself is administered in a request for letters.[15]

In each of the three stories something of bliss is described but in none is it real. Henry's feeling is intense but too young; it is a childish dream. For Bertha, the "bliss" is also an illusion, an effort of an older but nonetheless emotionally immature woman to attain to a feeling she does not have. The nameless narrator of "Poison" is simply deceived by his lack of experience. In "Poison," at the point of Beatrice's grossest lie—that she will not leave him—the narrator calls his condition "bliss." Ironically, trying to laugh it off, he says, "You sound as if you were saying good-bye," as, of course, she is. This irony is the assertion of all Miss Mansfield's descriptions of lovers: at the moment when they most hope they are approaching deep feelings of union, they are, instead, saying good-by, discovering their immutable separateness.

III

Undeceivably separate in the circumstances of their lives are Miss Mansfield's isolatoes, Ada Moss of "Pictures," Miss Brill, Ma Parker, and that inutterably stifled Robert Salesby of "The Man Without a Temperament." But all except Robert Salesby, who is not alone, reach out for some communication, and, in different ways, all fail.

To everyone in the Pension Villa Excelsior except his wife, Salesby is a frozen Englishman. She, a sickly invalid, responds with vital interest to the lush beauty of their surroundings and to the activities of people, those in the *pension* and the friends who write her from abroad, but Salesby sees nothing, thrusts his mail into his pocket, admits awareness of no one's feelings except his own. In his moments of respite from caring for his wife, a duty he carries out punctiliously, aggressively, but laconically, he focuses intently upon his homesickness. He shuts out the present world in vivid recollections of the past, when his wife was well and they were in England. Deep withdrawal is evident in that he thinks of her as Jinnie in his meditations, but in the present time of the story she is unnamed. Snow and rain he recalls with pleasure. But, when from his hotel balcony he could see a sky "the colour of jade . . . many stars; an enormous white moon" and distant lightning, he stares at the balcony rail. Walking "past the finest villas in the town, magnificent palaces, palaces worth coming any distance to see," he stares straight ahead. Twisting his ring (his symbolic fetter) as if he masochistically tormented a wound, he seems to mark time until the two-years' exile for his wife's health shall be ended. And she, recognizing his state, twists his ring, too.

He has come with her because she regarded him as "bread and wine," words he recalls as he recalls the doctor's unhappy verdict. But his nourishment, so fully yet so remotely administered, has rendered her apologetic, insecure, grasping at his slightest gestures to find some warmth in him. Pressed by her for an affirmation, he provides it in a typically negative word, "Rot!" This last word of the story encompasses the corruption of their love: his view of his own position and their relationship, yet his almost submerged will to survive this damnation.

For despite the negations apparent in the views of those who do not know Salesby, and in the aridity of his actions in the present time, his interior monologues reveal a former aliveness which indicates the author's sympathy even as she criticizes. But the final feeling is complex, for, though it is not London, life is brilliantly available on this Italian Riviera: Robert need not, as his name indicates, sail by; he need not rot, but he does.[16]

The other isolatoes are women alone; as noted by Simone de Beauvoir, they are a recurrent Mansfield fascination. Chronologically, the desperation of these women increases. In "Pictures," recast in 1919 from a 1917 version, Ada Moss seeks support in the despairing compromise of prostitution. In late 1920 Miss Brill is crushingly jolted, by a stranger's comment, from her comforting projections into companionship. Ma Parker's anguish must remain unexpressed for the most desolate reason: not only would her telling of the tale disturb the indifferent universe, but she can find no place even to weep.

Ranging from second-rate artist through impoverished gentlewoman to lowly, uneducated, old cleaning woman, these stories increase in painful effect. Ada Moss, though down and out, remains jaunty and continues to act, even if in her own defeat. Physically she is somewhat comic. Miss Brill, however, despite her inaccuracies, engages the reader's affection for her bright, sensitive enjoyment of the world/she fabricates in the Jardins Publiques. When her "hierarchy of unrealities." [17] is shattered, her only diversion from dull weekday work and her pleasure in her shabby fur-piece—in sum, her joy—have been taken away/The catastrophic descent from illusory pleasure is intensified by being revealed from her viewpoint. No distancing of emotion is allowed as the reader follows her train of thought and feeling. She has smiled, albeit tearfully and sentimentally, at the notion of a communion in song in the park. Stalwartly she has not merely stared like those "funny" ones she has noticed: "They were odd, silent, nearly all old, and from the way they stared they looked as though they'd just come from dark little rooms or even—cupboards!" The reader but not Miss Brill sees the similarity to her fur-piece. But after the callous boy, "the hero," reiteratively dwells on "that stupid old thing" and "her silly old mug," she creeps off home and conclusively recognizes her true kinship: "She . . . went into the little dark room—her room like a cupboard." When she packs away the fur-piece and "thought she heard something crying," her identification with that object is so complete that the reader fears she weeps and yet is too valiant to acknowledge it. Painfully, the reader also fears that perhaps for the last time she has "rubbed the life back into the dim little eyes."

Expressing her affection for Miss Brill, Miss Mansfield told Murry, "One writes (*one* reason why is) because one does care so passionately that one *must* show it—one must declare one's love." [18] That it was her mode of expressing faith is evident in her description of the mood in which she composed the story: "Last night I walked about and saw the new moon with the old moon in her arms and the lights in the water and the hollow pools full of stars—and lamented there was no God. But I came in and wrote *Miss Brill* instead; which is my insect Magnificat now and always." [19] In her perpetuation of awareness of Miss Brill's inmost nature, Miss Mansfield herself makes the statement of the pear tree outside Bertha Young's window.

In September, 1921, Miss Mansfield copied into a notebook the final passages of Chekhov's story "Misery" and added, "I would see every single French short story up the chimney for this. It's one of the masterpieces of the world."[20] She had written one of very similar approach in "The Life of Ma Parker." It, with "The Lady's Maid," provides two studies of isolation in servants. "The Lady's Maid" poured out the story of her life, shriveled by the will of her mistress, in a monologue which implied the presence of a kind guest who listened long past bedtime. Ma Parker met only embarrassed indifference in the literary gentleman she served. In this, Miss Mansfield goes Chekhov one better. His bereft Iona seeks sympathy for the death of his son first from his cab fares, a military officer, and three abusive, bad-tempered young men; then from a doorman; and finally from a fellow cabman who falls asleep. "Ordinary" people are conventionally expected to make ordinary, insensitive responses. But Ma Parker's literary gentleman, who by his very trade should be empathetic, is only patronizing and later parsimonious, as he badgers his hired "hag" about a teaspoon of cocoa. Ma Parker must review her life story to herself. Disaster after disaster goes through her mind as she cleans the flat. No one has ever seen her break down, but now, with the death of her grandson, she can bear no more, she wants to cry:

> If she could only cry now, cry for a long time, over everything, beginning with her first place and the cruel cook, going on to the doctor's, and then the seven little ones, death of her husband, the children's leaving her, and all the years of misery that led up to Lennie. But to have a proper cry over all these things would take a long time. All the same, the time for it had come. She must do it. She couldn't put it off any longer; she couldn't wait any more. . . . Where could she go?

Again her situation is worse than the one Chekhov portrayed. Iona at last seeks out his horse and tells the whole story. But for Ma Parker in her extremity there is not even a place for weeping. The gentleman's flat is out of the question. At home she would frighten her daughter. In public she would be reprimanded by a policeman. Her plight is not only isolation, but utter inability to relieve her pain by any means.

IV

The failure of love between human beings, the swift passing of beauty, and the indifference which prevents communication—these were the painful themes of Miss Mansfield's maturity. In December, 1920, she recorded her intention to go beyond these views:

> I should like this to be accepted as my confession.
> There is no limit to human suffering. When one thinks: ". . . —now I can go no deeper," one goes deeper. And so it is forever. . . . Suffering is boundless, it is eternity.
>
> . . . .
>
> One must *submit*. . . . Be overwhelmed. Accept it fully. Make it *part of life*.
> Everything in life that we really accept undergoes a change. So suffering must become Love. This is the mystery. . . . I must pass from personal love . . . to greater love. I must give to the whole of life what I gave to him.
>
> . . . .
>
> I must turn to *work*. I must put my agony into something, change it. "Sorrow shall be changed into joy."
> It is to lose oneself more utterly, to love more deeply, to feel oneself part of life—not separate.[21]

The turn did not come immediately. She had yet to write, early in 1921, "The Life of Ma Parker." Then she lay dormant, ill and exhausted, for several months. But in July the creative spurt began, and she wrote eleven stories by the end of January. She tapped now the vein of her truest love: seven of the stories were laid in New Zealand. With several of them she was very much dissatisfied. But in the brief time of September and October she wrote three memorable stories, "At the Bay," "The Garden-Party," and "The Doll's House." These stories pursue the consideration of order begun in "Prelude"; however, the writer is determined upon acceptance. Nothing of the caustic Miss Mansfield remains. Death has become part of order, and ugliness is no longer overwhelming. The dominant tone and organization of attitudes suggests an affirmation.

In "At the Bay" there are many passages which dwell with fondness on the quality of the living. Stanley, with all his foibles—his little selfishnesses, his materialism, his lack of imagination—is a man to love, and the cool Linda, who still rejects her children, fears childbearing, and remains aloof from most of life, does love Stanley. She herself has become a more sympathetic character and life exudes its radiance in the grandmother, in Mrs. Stubbs, and especially in the children.

The debate between order and disorder is first manifest between Stanley and Jonathan as they bathe in the sea. Stanley is going to work and has "no time to—to—to fool about." Jonathan speculates on his tension and makes his own avowal:

There was something pathetic in [Stanley's] determination to make a job of everything. . . . That was the way to live [like the sea]—carelessly, recklessly, spending oneself. . . . To take things easy, not to fight against the ebb and flow of life, but to give way to it—that was what was needed. It was this tension that was all wrong. To live—to live.

But once out of the sea, because he has stayed in too long, Jonathan is cold and tense himself, "as though some one was wringing the blood out of him." With ironic immediacy, he has yielded in this change of mood to the ebb and flow.

Later he expresses to Linda his hatred for his routine job: ". . . I'm like an insect that's flown into a room of its own accord. I dash against the walls, dash against the windows, flop against the ceiling, do everything on God's earth, in fact, except fly out again. And all the while I'm thinking . . . 'The shortness of life! The shortness of life!'" But he cannot escape from the order against which he rebels so violently. Why? Because ". . . it's not allowed, it's forbidden, it's against the insect law, to stop banging and flopping and crawling up the pane even for an instant." Then "in a changed voice, as if he were confiding a secret," he tells Linda the real reason: "Weak. . . . No stamina. No anchor. No guiding principle. . . ." Paradoxically, he cannot challenge order because nothing holds him fast in the ebb and flow; he has no order in himself. Yet in this story dominated by the image of the sea, there is a continual changing of positions among the characters. Jonathan too can stand for order. When he seeks his children in the evening, he is for a moment a frightening face looking out of the dark through the washhouse window. The orderly game becomes a chaos of fear. But then the door opens and he is revealed, Uncle Jonathan, the comforting representative of adult order.

In Stanley's tensions the same paradox emerges. Exceedingly neat and conscious of time, he appears at the breakfast table. The twenty-five minutes until the coach arrives are spent demanding services to which he is clearly accustomed. Order for Stanley means disorder for the household. Even Alice, the servant girl, is pulled into the hunt for his walking stick. All the women are thankful when he is gone. Linda compares the experience to "living in a house that couldn't be cured of the habit of catching on fire, on a ship that got wrecked every day."

Apparently, too, Stanley's behavior ebbs and flows, for Linda also knows "a timid, sensitive, innocent Stanley who knelt down every night to say his prayers, and who longed to be good." This is a loyal, honest, simple man, who suffers at any deceit from those he believes in. Then, like Jonathan, Stanley is imaged as a "trapped beast," wildness growing distraught at a violation of his order. For his is a wrong kind of order, order involving tension.

The children play at being beasts, kept in order by the rules of the game as laid down by Pip. Secure in this pattern, they have escaped the excessive order of the Samuel Joseph children, for whose undisciplined natures an "awful" daily program is planned and administered by their lady-help, complete with police whistle. Only Kezia runs counter to the conventions. Despite protests, she is a bee, an insect (like Jonathan) rather than an animal. And to help Lottie, who is too young to play well, she delays the game, playing without the usual competitive spirit. Kezia's sympathies are such that she challenges order for the sake of joy. In a scene of more serious content, near in time to the story's high noon, Kezia, learning from her grandmother that it is in the order of events that they should both someday die, protests:

"*You're* not to die." Kezia was very decided.

. . . .

"Promise me you won't ever do it, grandma," pleaded Kezia.
The old woman went on knitting.
"Promise me! Say never."
But still her grandma was silent.

But the seriousness and anxiety ebb to a tickling match, after which "Both of them had forgotten what the 'never' was about."

Again, in Kezia's case, order and disorder are sometimes one. Beryl scolds her for messy eating, and sister Isabel agrees that "Only babies play with their food." But Kezia feels that "she had only dug a river down the middle of her porridge, filled it, and was eating the banks away." To her it is an order. And Kezia's self-esteem builds for her a tensionless order.

A comical merging of order and disorder occurs at Mrs. Stubbs's shop:

On the veranda there hung a long string of bathing dresses, clinging together as though they'd just been rescued from the sea . . . and beside them there hung a cluster of sand-shoes so extraordinarily mixed that to get at one pair you had to tear apart and forcibly separate at least fifty. . . . The two windows, arranged in the form of precarious pyramids, were crammed so tight, piled so high, that it seemed only a conjuror could prevent them from toppling over.

Mrs. Stubbs, looking "like a friendly brigand," welcomes the restrained and proper Alice "so warmly that she found it quite difficult to keep up her 'manners.' They consisted of persistent little coughs and hems, pulls at her gloves, tweaks at her skirt, and a curious difficulty in seeing what was set before her or understanding what was said." As they shout to be heard above a roaring Primus, the display of Mrs. Stubbs's new photographs is broad, chaotic comedy:

Mrs. Stubbs sat in an arm-chair, leaning very much to one side. There was a look of mild astonishment on her large face, and well there might be. For though the arm-chair stood on a carpet, to the left of it, miraculously skirting the carpet-border, there was a dashing waterfall. On her right stood a Grecian pillar with a giant fern-tree on either side of it, and in the background towered a gaunt mountain, pale with snow. "It's a nice style, isn't it?" shouted Mrs. Stubbs. . . .

To end the scene, she advises Alice that "Freedom's best," and Alice, with typical rigidity, recoils: "Freedom! Alice gave a loud, silly little titter. She felt awkward. Her mind flew back to her own kitching. Ever so queer! She wanted to be back in it again."

At the approximate center of the story, near the noon of its single day in which time is so carefully noted from before dawn into darkness,[22] Linda explores the mystery that is life and emerges with a more affirmative view than that found in "Prelude." Her focal position, at the high point of story time in "At the Bay," probably indicates the importance of her conclusions, and she will in the end receive some implicit confirmation from the all-enveloping sea.

Examining the beauty of the flowers and musing on their swift mutability, Linda asks the crucial question: "Why, then, flower at all? Who takes the trouble—or the joy—to make all these things that are wasted, wasted. . . . It was uncanny." [Miss Mansfield's dots] She does not recognize it yet, but the immediate answer, her baby boy, lies beside her on the grass, his head turned away, asleep. That her question involves, more seriously than for Kezia, the fear of her own death appears in her next consideration of the flowers:

If only one had time to look at these flowers long enough, time to get over the sense of novelty and strangeness, time to know them! But as soon as one paused to part the petals, to discover the underside of the leaf, along came Life and one was swept away. . . . Along came Life like a wind and she was seized and shaken; she had to go. . . . Was there no escape?

Her life appears to be spent on calming the excited Stanley Burnell and fearing childbirth, the latter made worse because "she did not love her children."

But as this thought runs through her mind, she discovers that the boy is awake. He smiles, and Linda finds her answer:

There was something so quaint, so unexpected about that smile that Linda smiled herself. But she checked herself and said to the boy coldly, "I don't like babies."
"Don't like babies?" The boy couldn't believe her. "Don't like me?" He waved his arms foolishly at his mother.
Linda dropped off her chair on to the grass.
"Why do you keep on smiling?" she said severely.
. . . .
Linda was so astonished at the confidence of this little creature. . . . Ah no, be sincere. That was not what she felt; it was something far

different, it was something so new, so. . . . The tears danced in her eyes; she breathed in a small whisper to the boy, "Hallo, my funny!" [Miss Mansfield's dots]

Out of the order of things which brings forth children in pain and fades the flowers too soon Linda finds at last that her reward is the brief beauty of love. Her acceptance has not lessened when later in the evening she listens to Jonathan's unhappy and futile rebellion. Observing the beauty of evening, she or the author (it is not clear here which) recognizes that a cruel meaning may linger in sunset:

Sometimes when those beams of light show in the sky they are very awful. They remind you that up there sits Jehovah, the jealous God, the Almighty, Whose eye is upon you. . . . You remember that at His coming the whole world will shake into one ruined graveyard; the cold, bright angels will drive you this way and that, and there will be no time to explain what could be explained so simply. . . . [Miss Mansfield's dots]

Linda's final thought, however, is different: "But to-night it seemed to Linda there was something infinitely joyful and loving in those silver beams. And now no sound came from the sea. It breathed softly as if it would draw the tender, joyful beauty into its own bosom." The ebb and flow continues as Jonathan interrupts with, "It's all wrong, it's all wrong," but his voice is shadowy. For Linda, the question is answered.

But Miss Mansfield, agreeing with Chekhov that a writer poses questions but does not answer them, devotes the last incident to Beryl's exploration. All day Beryl has experimented with disorder and ugliness, but she herself appears to prefer order and is repelled by the evil she encounters. Her experience at the beach with Mrs. Harry Kemper parallels that in the evening with Mr. Harry Kemper. These two are so alike that, when swimming, Beryl sees with horror that the unattractive, disorderly woman looks "like a horrible caricature of her husband," who, nonetheless, is "so handsome that he looked like a mask. . . ." The ebb-and-flow mingling of freedom and repression characterizes both incidents. The tense, "burnt out" Mrs. Kemper flouts the conventions of the summer resort and urges the inhibited Beryl to freedom: "I believe in pretty girls having a good time. . . . Enjoy yourself." But as they undress for swimming, it is Mrs. Kemper, not Beryl, who is seen to have bound her body in corset stays.

That Beryl's chance to "enjoy herself" should be offered by Mr. Kemper is an apt irony. As the adventure begins, Beryl, in a romantic reverie in her room, feels the disorder of darkness. She is a "conspirator" before she sees a strange man, perhaps a burglar, in the garden. Having recognized him, she refuses his invitation on conventional, orderly grounds, but his challenge lures her outside. When he forcibly embraces her, constraining her to a freedom, she, repelling it, "wrenched free."

The sea serves many purposes throughout the story. It is the scene of Stanley's conflict with Jonathan, Beryl's adventure with Mrs. Kemper, and the children's play. Though it creates natural beauty, the final experiences of all whose feelings are described in contact with the sea are unpleasant. Rewarded at first, Stanley and Jonathan leave it tense. Beryl, aware of the warm blue, silver, and golden beauty, sees Mrs. Kemper as a rat in the sea and feels the woman's poison enter her there. Even little Lottie, "when a bigger wave than usual, an old whiskery one, came lolloping along in her direction, . . . scrambled to her feet with a face of horror and flew up the beach again." Around high noon, just after Linda has attained acceptance of the order of life and death and just before Kezia will challenge death with laughter, the beach is deserted, but under the fiery sun the sea reveals a reflected but mysterious world. It is as though the sea, which Linda who attains the only insight of the story never goes near, would maintain somehow, in its ebb and flow, its secret and its tension. The order, in fact, of the sea is a disorder.

Final comment, then, is left to the sea. The isolated emphasis that is the single, short paragraph of Section 13 implies that it pictures the alternate rise and fall of emotion, negation and affirmation of attitude throughout the story: "A cloud, small, serene, floated across the moon. In that moment of darkness the sea sounded deep, troubled. Then the cloud sailed away, and the sound of the sea was a vague murmur, as though it waked out of a dark dream. All was still."

The sea has dominated the entire story. In the opening all the land is enveloped, hidden by "sea-mist." The first section is like the overture to a piece of music, as a shepherd, his dog, and a flock of sheep appear out of the mist. The shepherd whistles, smokes a pipe, then whistles again as he disappears. The sheep bleat and are answered by ghostly herds under the sea. Florrie, the Burnell's cat, and the only member of the resort colony to see this passage, arches her back at the dog, who sensibly ignores her. None of these characters appear again except Florrie, but they have suggested, as the opening bars should, the basic themes of the composition. The dog and the shepherd are responsible order among the feckless sheep, and they are very much at ease, very relaxed in the world in which they perform their task. They are order without tension, the ideal natural order, probably the order of acceptance and love which Linda discovers.

Florrie's reappearance in Section 11 acts as a musical motif to recall the images and feeling of the opening, to effect a return of the mind to that tranquillity just as Stanley, much subdued but still expressing his tensions, returns. The Stanley and Linda theme is resolved peacefully; there is the excited flurry of Beryl's section; and then the coda, back where Florrie has pointed the way, with the sea and the closing direction.

Far less complicated in structure and, perhaps for that reason, more immediately moving are the acceptances of "The Garden-Party" and "The Doll's House." In "The Garden-Party" Laura's struggle against convention and her uneasy search for her role is made clear by her disposal of the bread and butter she takes to the lawn at the beginning of the day. She carries it out in a moment of reckless joy at the beauty, excitement, and promise of the day. She hides it from the workmen, fearing to be thought childish. Then, as her fellow-feeling grows, she eats it in big bites, imagining herself like "a work girl."

She is trying to discover right behavior, and she suspects uneasily that it is not to be found in what is conventionally correct. She does not feel, before the haggard look of a pale workman, that it is right to have a band for their party. Her suggestions for the location of the marquée are wrong, but the right place conceals the lovely karaka-trees. Her more intense notion that the party should be stopped because a man has been killed is called absurd and extravagant by the practical sister Jose, and it first amuses and then annoys her mother. Later she is sure that to take the remains of the party food to the bereaved family is wrong, and is again overruled. "Run down just as you are," bids her mother, airily unaware of the feelings of the poor, and Laura goes, awkwardly embarrassed by the mission, by her party dress, and by her hat.

It is the hat which distracted her from her protest against the party, just as Pat's earrings distracted a younger Kezia from a protest against death in "Prelude." So it is appropriate that before the dead young man, to whom she must say something, Laura says, "Forgive my hat." This incongruous remark at the moment of Laura's greatest seriousness and greatest childishness (she "gave a loud childish sob") renders her view of the body convincing where it might otherwise have seemed a frivolous sentimentality or mere bathos. Seeing the young man as "wonderful, beautiful . . . this marvel," she tries to communicate the experience to her brother. As death and the party have existed side by side, so do her exaltation and her tears. Again the menace has merged with and become beauty.

In a letter of March 13, 1922, Miss Mansfield commented on the insight which Laura struggles to make articulate:

The diversity of life and how we try to fit in everything, Death included. That is bewildering for a person of Laura's age. She feels things ought to happen differently. . . . But life isn't like that. We haven't the ordering of it. Laura says, "But all these things must not happen at once." And Life answers, "Why not? . . ." And they *do* all happen, it is inevitable. And it seems to me there is beauty in that inevitability. [Miss Mansfield's dots] [23]

"The Doll's House" is Miss Mansfield's last portrait of Kezia, who, as always, in her misbehavior does the right thing. She grants a brief vision of the doll's lamp to the cruelly despised and derided Kelvey children, and they are alert enough to grasp its beauty despite the angry and frightening words of Beryl. When Kezia had announced in the schoolyard that the little lamp was best of all, "nobody paid any attention." But though she had no time to point it out to the Kelveys, after they have fled, Else, whom "nobody had ever seen . . . smile" and who rarely spoke, does smile and speak. In her soft words, "I seen the little lamp," is affirmation rising from the simplest, most helplessly wretched level that Katherine Mansfield will describe. The writer has come far from the little boy's wailing in "Sun and Moon" at the melted, broken ice-cream house. By a strenuous effort of will and imagination, she defied for a time all of the negative pressures laid upon her by ill health and by personal failures in her relationship with Murry. In the years of strain leading, she suspected, to her dying, she hopefully proclaimed that there was beauty in any ugliness—even in death.

CHAPTER 6

"Will There Be a Ripple . . . ?"

I

IT REMAINS to describe the final artistry of Katherine Mansfield in terms of three stories which manifest her technique brought to a fine finish and her attitudes expressed at their greatest depth. In the late months of 1920, while exploring the theme of isolation, she wrote "The Stranger" and "The Daughters of the Late Colonel." "The Fly," her next to last completed story, was composed in February, 1922, while she underwent treatment for tuberculosis.

These three episodes of discovery embody the typical Mansfield work. The subject in each is people who suffer some emotional loss. In each instance the characters are affected by a death, but it becomes clear that this death is not central in the author's mind; she celebrates, instead, spiritual death in her main characters, death of which none of them is completely aware. All of these stories are, in Miss Mansfield's phrase, "a cry against corruption" —specifically against failure of the spirit.

The action is typically slight: a man visits with a friend, then kills a fly; a man meets his wife's ship, takes her to a hotel, and is disheartened by her account of a shipboard experience; two women try vaguely to organize their affairs after the death of their father. The most complicated structure, that of "The Daughters of the Late Colonel," surrounds the least action. The other two are largely chronological in order, though in "The Stranger" Janey tells briefly of the death of the young man and in "The Fly" Woodifield tells of his daughters' trip to Belgium and the boss recalls briefly his son's participation in the business. Both these stories open on highly particularized scenes and are immediately focused in the consciousness of the protagonist, after which the narrator has little access to any other awareness. "The Daughters of the Late Colonel" is a virtuoso piece in the use of multipersonal viewpoint.

Since the tone of the narrator is that of the interior monologues, it is difficult to locate a purely narrative segment in any of the stories. The treatment is dramatic, with summary or generalization avoided by the author. The reader must infer from the gestures and the speech of the characters what their natures are and what Miss Mansfield means to convey. She builds her stories toward such moments of discovery. John Hammond and the colonel's daughters announce what they have realized, but the boss can reach no conclusion. In each case, the implicit revelation is greater for the reader than for the characters. The dramatic effect is increased by this irony of a more accurate knowledge in the audience, a knowledge, however, which the author does not define.

"The Stranger" describes the death of the heart of John Hammond, who discovers that, as he has feared, his wife is not wholly his own. She extends a tenderness that he feels is denied him not only to their children, whom he rivals, but to a dying stranger. The reader discovers that they, too, are strangers: Hammond, who wants too much of a wife, and Janey, who does not completely understand his need.

The two men involved in this story are parallel in that one apparently died of feelings similar to the other's, agitation at the homecoming. The young stranger died of a weak heart. Janey explains, "He had a severe attack in the afternoon—excitement— nervousness, I think, about arriving. And after that he never recovered." In the first segment of the story Hammond wins the reader's sympathy by his excitement as he paces the wharf, waiting for his wife's ship to dock. His warmth toward the others waiting is egocentrically caused by his assumption that Janey's arrival somehow means something to them, too. He tries to divert a child from her hunger for tea, paces, chats affably, and finally gives away all his cigars because he sees his wife on the approaching ship. As the ship turns, he cannot tell "whether that deep throbbing was her engines or his heart. . . . He had to nerve himself to bear it, whatever it was." The end of the story implies that Hammond, like the other stranger, never recovered.

But Hammond's metaphorical death results from his intensely

possessive feeling; he wants more than can be demanded of an individual. There are many evidences that he knows this. When he embraces Janey in her cabin, "again, as always, he had the feeling he was holding something that never was quite his—his." In the hotel he says, "I feel I'll never have you to myself again," and this is his conclusion upon her revelation of the stranger's death in her arms. Even with her at last in his arms, his interior monologue, which recounts most of the story, reveals his insecurity: "But just as when he embraced her he felt she would fly away, so Hammond never knew—never knew for dead certain that she was as glad as he was. . . . Would he always have this craving—this pang like hunger, somehow, to make Janey so much part of him that there wasn't any of her to escape? He wanted to blot out everybody, everything." His feelings are rendered as understandably pathetic, but they lead him to self-exile.

The reader is very soon certain that Janey is not so glad as her husband at their meeting, for they are, from the beginning, at cross-purposes. Seeing her from afar, Hammond must turn to his cigar case to compose himself, but, when he looks again, she is "talking to some woman and at the same time watching him, ready for him." At his warm greeting, she meets him with a "cool little voice" and a "half-smile." He brushes aside her concern for the children, and he has left at the hotel their letters, which she would like immediately. Later, in the hotel, he selfishly fails to understand that she would like to read these letters, and even resents them, "tucked into her frilled blouse" and rustling there when he has her on his knee. He is in a rush to get her away from the ship, but she must make her polite farewells to fellow passengers, the captain, and the doctor. His feeling that "he'd got her" is belied when, in the cab, after a bit she "gently drew her hand away." Even by the removal of her hat she delays coming to sit on Hammond's knees, and, though then she lies on his breast, he feels her so remote that he must demand, "Kiss me, Janey! You kiss me." But this too is not adequate. To him it seems that her kiss "confirmed what they were saying, signed the contract. But that wasn't what he wanted; that wasn't at all what he thirsted for."

When they entered the hotel room, the fire Hammond had ordered was blazing, as was his passion. As Janey begins to explain the delay in docking, she and Hammond watch the fire die. The sequence of fire images accompanies his emotional death and echoes a tonal foreshadowing against which he had protested on the dock. He noted then the coming darkness and waved his umbrella as though to keep it off. "But the dusk came slowly, spreading like a slow stain over the water." In their room "The flames hurried—hurried over the coals, flickered, fell." Janey tells her story of the death of the young man.

When she reveals, "He died in my arms," the effect on Hammond is like that of the stranger's heart attack: "The blow was so sudden that Hammond thought he would faint. He couldn't move; he couldn't breathe. He felt all his strength flowing—flowing into the big dark chair." Unaware, Janey continues, and his response intensifies: "Ah, my God, what was she saying! What was she doing to him! This would kill him!" Snow images, mingled with the dying fire, image his feelings. As Janey ends her story and is silent,

her words, so light, so soft, so chill, seemed to hover in the air, to rain into his breast like snow.
The fire had gone red. Now it fell with a sharp sound and the room was colder. Cold crept up his arms. The room was huge, immense, glittering. It filled his whole world. There was the great blind bed, with his coat flung across it like some headless man saying his prayers. There was the luggage, ready to be carried away again, anywhere. . . .

Here, in full stride, Katherine Mansfield carries the technique of poetry into the short story. The images convey the empty, frozen, disintegrated quality of Hammond's realization.

But Janey, a stranger to her stranger, cannot or will not understand his attitude. She wonders at him. At his moan ". . . why *you?*" she "turned quickly, quickly searched his face. 'You don't *mind*, John, do you?' she asked. 'You don't—It's nothing to do with you and me.'" But she senses his drop in mood and asks again, "You're not—sorry I told you, John darling? It hasn't made you sad? It hasn't spoilt our evening—our being alone together?"

When Janey first told him that a young man had died at sea, Hammond was uneasy: "It was in some queer way, as though he and Janey had met a funeral on their way to the hotel." Now he receives her account as if it were his own funeral. At her doubtful question, in his mind the tragedy is completed. He tells himself: "They would never be alone together again." He is crushed, paradoxically, by his recognition of what he has always suspected: he cannot, no matter how well he plans the occasion, ever have total possession of Janey. Whether he is right or wrong in his appraisal, he cannot communicate his pain to her. Thus they remain strangers, neither understanding the other. The antithetic "alone together" describes their permanent situation, past and present.

Miss Mansfield sympathized completely with her characters, but she did not consider their plight tragic. While composing, she reported to Murry that she was in a "black mood": "*I am writing. . . .* and until this story is finished I am engulfed. It's not a tragic story either. . . ." But it possessed her: "I've *been* this man, *been* this woman. . . . I've been a seagull hovering at the stern and a hotel porter whistling through his teeth. . . . one IS the spectacle for the time."[1]

Despite her avowed empathy, she limits herself as an author. Opening the story as the omniscient author, she shifts the viewpoint into the consciousness of John Hammond with the words "But what a fool—" From that moment on, the author may reveal a little more of Hammond's consciousness than he himself recognizes, but largely the story is seen through his eyes. The ironic truth of his first words about himself indicates the author's view of his character: his misery is of his own making because of his lack of understanding. In the opening scene he is only lamenting his lack of field glasses and his resulting inability to see Janey on the ship, but his failure is a greater one: he cannot *see* Janey no matter how close he gets. When, in his arms, she tells of the stranger who died in hers, his response reveals to the reader that they are also strangers and yet that it need not be. In this, John Hammond is, as he said, a fool, a pathetically mistaken man.

"The Daughters of the Late Colonel" are pathetically wasted women, but Miss Mansfield has described their condition, because it is absurd, in a series of comic scenes. Josephine and Constantia, two middle-aged women[2] who have spent their lives taking care of an irascible father and keeping out of his way, have been so intimidated by the experience that after his death they are unable to cope with his nurse and the maid. Their timidity extends to being unable to believe that the colonel is really dead. As a result, their tentative efforts to make decisions or to take practical action are often hilarious.

Many jokes rise from the funeral situation. Constantia, always ready with an inappropriate word, hopes for "a good one that will last." Josephine panics at the cemetery because they have buried Father without his permission and she is certain that "he was bound to find out sooner or later." She even imagines him complaining about the bills. Constantia reassures her: "We couldn't have kept him, Jug—we couldn't have kept him unburied. At any rate, not in a flat that size." But fantastically Josephine feels that they "ought to have tried to, just for a time at least," and she is sure that he will never forgive them. Equally absurd is their fear of disturbing his room, which becomes a conviction that he is in the chest of drawers "ready to spring." Constantia triumphs on this occasion. "Why shouldn't we be weak for once in our lives, Jug? . . . It's much nicer to be weak than to be strong," she says and boldly locks the wardrobe.

An extended memory of a scene at tea with their nephew Cyril, which culminates in a ridiculous attempt to make the deaf colonel hear that Cyril's father "is still very fond of meringues," characterizes these women as inept but hopeful in dealing with their bullying father. Their efforts to please Cyril are, of course, rendered more pathetic by his youthful, rushed lack of appreciation.

Eleven sections of the story characterize them as amusingly fearful, mild, kind women. In the twelfth, at the sound of a barrel-organ, they jump, still under their father's spell, to send the organ-grinder away, and suddenly realization comes: they need never stop him again; they will never again hear their father pounding his stick and giving angry orders. They smile strangely and hear the barrel-organ play, "*It will never thump again. . . . A week since father died.*" Supported by images of music and increasing sunlight, they ponder and for a moment reach out toward some future change in their situation. But it is a sunlight which "thieved its way in," a "thieving sun" which will not win them. Each starts to speak her thoughts; thus, by their interruptions, they stop one another. Neither will continue, but the scene with the wardrobe, where Constantia knew what was in her sister's mind, implies that she knows here as well. "Don't be absurd, Con," says Josephine, and each implores the other to speak. But they are absurd. They are like the sparrows Josephine heard, whose "queer little crying noise" she knew was inside her. They are like the mouse Constantia felt so sorry for that she couldn't "think how they manage to live at all." These animal images in the beginning and end of the story unify it and spell out their doom, as the sun is symbolically replaced by a cloud. Both assert they have forgotten what they wished to say, but this is only credible in the case of the vague Constantia. With Josephine it seems a practical denial. As Miss Mansfield explained in a letter, after that moment of turning toward the sun, "they died as surely as Father was dead." [3]

The virtuosity of the story lies in the treatment of time and point of view. The omniscient author is withdrawn but, as in "Prelude" (to which Miss Mansfield declared this one akin in form), is free to penetrate into any consciousness in the story. Most of the narrative unfolds through the mind of one sister or the other, but sometimes their likeness is stressed by a composite viewpoint, which can split with ease. As they talk of sending their father's watch to Benny in Ceylon, Josephine points out that it would be carried by runners: "Both paused to watch a black man in white linen drawers running through the pale fields for dear life, with a large brown-paper parcel in his hands. Josephine's black man was tiny; he scurried along glistening like an ant. But there was something blind and tireless about Constantia's tall, thin fellow, which made him, she decided, a very unpleasant person indeed. . . . On the veranda . . . stood Benny." [The first set of dots is Miss Mansfield's] Their minds move together, part in a manner that characterizes them, and join again. Consistently Constantia seems to know what Josephine is talking about, even when she introduces a subject abruptly. It is an evidence of their long, secluded life together, but it is also technically necessary in order to ready the reader for the climactic penetration into their longings, which are individual but complementary.

Time seems at the mercy of these minds wandering into the past and vaguely into fantasies of the future, but it is, in fact, well under the narrator's control. Though a week is impressionistically described, Sections 6 through 12 take place on the last day—the Saturday after the colonel's death. Section 5 occurs on Thursday, while Sections 3 (where its time becomes specific) and 4 are on the Saturday, one taking up morning, one afternoon. Only the first two sections and part of the third are generalized to suggest typical behavior during the week and thus to contribute the aura of bemused muddle which is the essential tone of the women through whose minds most of the events are seen.

During these segments of present story time there are recollections of the past: the colonel's single eye glaring in death, Mr. Farolles' offer of "a little Communion," Cyril's remarkable communication at tea, efforts to lay traps for the haughty maid Kate— all are ridiculous. The visions of the future are even more so: the colonel furious about his own funeral bills, the runner taking the watch to Benny, the plans for cooking should Kate be dismissed. Their vague, erratic circling reveals not only their history and characters but also their disability, their absurdity. The total view accords with their abandonment of any possible future change. The most revealing statement is the opening sentence of the story: "The week after [the colonel's death] was one of the busiest weeks of their lives." That it should be so is the mark of their utter deprivation.

With neither compassion nor humor, "The Fly" emerges as Katherine Mansfield's starkest view, her bitterest and almost her final cry against corruption. At its most obvious level, the events of the story are slight. The boss enjoys the admiring visit of an enfeebled old friend until the deaths of their sons are recalled. Alone, unable to summon the self-pity he has mistaken for grief, he diverts himself by tormenting to death a fly, but he is further depressed by this activity. He is clearly a bully and a sadist. The satisfactory docility of the remembered son, coupled with his guilt in looking at the boy's picture, leads one to suspect that his treatment of the fly reflects similar, though less extreme, behavior toward his son. He no doubt bullied the boy as he now bullies Macey and Woodifield. But the feeling persists that there must be more than the immediately perceived meaning in this much explicated story.

Miss Mansfield's notebooks, letters, and short stories are sprinkled, from 1918 on, with images of flies. It might be merely a visual description of a baby, as in "The Voyage"; of little boys dressed in black;[4] or an account of her own illness, as in the letters of 1918 and 1919.[5] She had felt herself to be a fly "dropped into the milk-jug and fished out again," and she had imaged

Jonathan Trout, who felt himself a victim of unknown forces, as an insect which could have been a fly.[6] It is not unlikely then that her own position in a losing conflict with ill-health, destiny, an insensitive father,[7] and even, since the fly is in the ink, the battle to meet short-story deadlines, are reflected at the biographical level in the story.

But if biographical readings are often dubious, how much more so for a writer who avowedly projects her being, for the literary moment, into every person or beast she describes. The meaning of the story may be more deeply plumbed within the fictional frame.

The likeness between old Mr. Woodifield and the boss goes beyond their mutual loss of sons in the war.[8] Neither has been to Belgium to visit the graves; both have apparently suffered deeply from grief; but, most significantly, both, when the thought of these deaths cross their minds, quickly forget.[9] It is not just doddering old Woodifield who cannot remember that he intended to mention his daughters' visit to their sons' graves, but the final sentence of the story emphasizes a similar lapse on the part of the robustly healthy boss: *"For the life of him* he could not remember."* [My italics] There is a double meaning here: not remembering seems to the boss to support his own vitality; but, to restore the life of his son, he would not be able to remember because he does not really wish to have that "stern-looking" young soldier take over the business and mastery that he himself possesses with such pleasure. He also does not wish to come, as has his near-double Woodifield, under the tutelage of his junior.[10]

The condition of Woodifield, which the boss enjoys in others but fears in himself, is clearly defined from the beginning: "he peered out of the great, green leather armchair . . . as a baby peers out of its pram." His voice is a weak piping. Others govern his behavior and even dress him. But, if he is a baby, the boss is little more: in the imagery of Miss Mansfield, he "rolled in his office chair, stout, rosy, five years older. . . ." He is a boy, a greedy boy,[11] whose new office furniture suggests treacle and sausages. And, like a boy, he torments the fly. In his good health he is no more manly than old Woodifield, but he is far more disturbing.

Through such a portrait of what Miss Mansfield had called in 1919 "the Boss Omnipotent" she flung her final defiance in his teeth. From the beginning her stories had asked, "What is it all for?" and the answer had only been "how *stupid.*" She was without belief in any superior force governing the affairs of men, but her protest here is made clear in anthropomorphic terms. The force, she would say, that creates and then destroys is materialistic, gross, motiveless. There is no transcendence, no glimmer of the ideal in the process of bloom and decay. But worse, there is immaturity, lack of depth, in the destructive pattern. The pattern is cruel.

The hope implicit in flowering intensifies the desolation of destruction. All the relationships of the story demonstrate this point. The boss has treated his son as he treated the fly, alternately assisting and encouraging, then crushing. In the rearing of boys such behavior is typically called "making a man of him," but the look of the man challenges the boss, so his grief at the loss is false. His treatment of Woodifield and Macey splits the two aspects of the bully's behavior or the pattern of life.[12] To Woodifield the boss is benevolent, giving him a taste of whisky, something "good for him." [13] Macey he has bullied until the old office worker is reduced to subhuman behavior, a doglike personality. "Look sharp" are the boss's words to both Macey and the fly.

But the feelings of the boss are involved in his behavior. He enjoys the visit of the enfeebled old man and the slavish nervousness of Macey. His empathy with the fly connects him symbolically with these men. The fly "cowed" is Macey; "timid and weak," it is Woodifield. Past grief has carried the boss through these stages, compelling him to stand in relation to the forces of life as the fly stands to himself. The author has placed him in a cyclic progression, the meaning of which he subconsciously senses. The boy, Macey, Woodifield, the fly, death are stages in a life sequence in which the boss has two places. His position as prime mover he enjoys; his identity with all of those who move toward death he prefers to forget.[14] A frightening reminder of his low degree is the "grinding feeling of wretchedness" which occurs when he kills the fly. It is an unwitting enactment of his own position. He destroys, but he is destroyed. On one level, it is a statement about the sadist; on another, a last description of the incomprehensible life pattern which feeds on its own destruction.

II

Katherine Mansfield was not a philosopher. Unlike some modern short-story writers, she neither followed nor formulated a system of thought, nor did she wish to. Her desire was to achieve purity of vision: to see clearly herself in order to transmit truth to the reader. Like Conrad, she wanted to make the reader *see*. But like Chekhov, she had no program; she made no recommendations; she presented problems but no solutions. To her the essential problem was just that absence of explanation.

Probably—at least, there is no evidence to the contrary—she never heard of existentialism, but her most consistent observation is of the absurdity that dominates life. So it rings out in her mature stories: isolation, unnecessary and often self-imposed; the capacity for life absurdly wasted; motiveless destruction which involves self-destruction. Her sympathy is limited for the individual who victimizes himself; in her view of the helpless she escapes the sentimentality of her early work to achieve a detachment that calls for comic treatment. She regretted her negation; she mitigated it in her affirmations of beauty; but she could never deny what she saw: in the end, usually too soon, beauty faded, joy bore an undertone of sadness, love was inadequately realized, order was an ebb and flow that involved disorder.

Shortly after her thirty-fourth birthday, sure that her attitude had been wrong and her selection of materials falsely controlled, she ceased to write and entered the Gurdjieff Institute for the Harmonious Development of Man at Fontainebleau. She hoped to "get into that real living simple truthful *full* life" that she had groped for in her notebooks. According to Murry and to conversations reported by Orage, the Institute did "purify" her, and she expected to begin writing again, a new kind of affirming story,[15] but death intervened.

Her spiritual and artistic dissatisfaction is an adjunct of her times. Since David Daiches' study, *The Novel and the Modern World*, it has become a commonplace to explain the technical experimentation of twentieth-century writing as a response to "the drying up of traditional sources of value and the consequent decay of uniform belief." In the absence of a public standard, the artist was obliged to rely on his own subjective selection of materials and then faced the problem of making that selection appear to reflect an objective standard of values. For Daiches, Katherine Mansfield is illustrative in her dependence on "a personal sense of truth" found through reliance on a highly cultivated sensitivity. Her "response to experience was such that she was able to extract, and present, the greatest significance from a very limited phase of it." [16]

Austin M. Wright's analysis of what distinguishes the traditional from the modern short story in America reads like a description, as he is aware, of a Mansfield work. In form, he finds the modern story reduced in magnitude, tending toward the static. In the much diminished plot, reversal, often muffled, has become "an illuminating moment in which the important constant in the static situation asserts itself." Dramatic effect is increased, in that the reader of the increasingly complex form often understands more than the protagonist. Wright explains the result:

These tendencies—the reduction of magnitude of action and the refinement of complexity—make possible the development of richer and more delicate effects within the confines of short-story length. . . . By using the small action, the illuminating episode, as a unifying principle, the writers of the twenties reduced the amount of activity or incident necessary to bring their stories to completion. Thus they had more scope for the development of character and thought. . . . [In this] attempt to sharpen and concentrate the focus of the short story . . . they brought [it] much closer to the nature of the lyric poem. [17]

He finds the significant forerunners in this mode to be Chekhov, Joyce, and Katherine Mansfield, and he notes their kinship in depicting "social disintegration and emotional isolation." [18]

Likewise Erich Auerbach sees the "distinctive characteristics of the realistic novel of the era between the two great wars . . . multipersonal representation of consciousness, time strata, disintegration of the continuity of exterior events, shifting of the narrative viewpoint" as symptoms of a confused, declining society. However, despite the frequent "impression of hopelessness" and "something hostile to the reality which they represent," he finds in the exploitation of the "random occurrence" and in its rendering in depth the discovery of the literary matter "which is comparatively independent of the controversial and unstable orders over which men fight and despair." [19] His analysis of these techniques and attitudes in Virginia Woolf's *To the Lighthouse* could as easily have resulted from a study of Miss Mansfield's "The Daughters of the Late Colonel."

The serious writer does not always self-consciously set out to reflect his age or to relieve it of its conflicts by some artistic formulation. He is part of a complex which he defines only in his artifact. His effort is, by the act of integration in creation, to relieve, if anyone, himself. Except in rare instances, usually when the artist has become critic and/or teacher, he has remained inarticulate or inaccurate in declarations about the larger significance of his work. The discreet man simply stands by what he has made.

Thus Katherine Mansfield—always dissatisfied with her work and at the end reaching out for some new breakthrough to greater "reality"—without a clear critical theory, reflected, as was inevitable, her era and provided solutions for writers who faced and would face similar problems. That her work was a dominant influence in the development of the modern short story is not debatable, though it may be an accident of time and publication history.

Her most important collections, *Bliss* and *The Garden-Party*, were published on both sides of the Atlantic in the first three years of the 1920's. The extent of interest in her work in 1923, the year of her death, is reflected in the need for three printings of *The Dove's Nest* by Knopf in the first three months of the book's existence. There is no doubt that John Middleton Murry exploited the interest created by her death. He managed to keep her before the public in his journal, the *Adelphi*, and abroad in the *Yale Review*, with two years of posthumous publication. By 1930 he had brought out eight volumes of writing that Miss Mansfield never intended for print. Again, when Knopf issued a complete collection, *The Short Stories of Katherine Mansfield* (September, 1937), a second printing was needed by November, a fifth by 1950. Miss Berkman has described the development of Miss Mansfield's "legend" as "a wash of sentiment that inundated the periodicals of England, America, and France." [20] But despite the intellectual and aesthetic inadequacy of Miss Mansfield's initial reception, her stories circulated. She was read widely, apparently by many who would also write.

It is difficult to insist on specific influences among writers of this period because they were all attacking similar materials and working out similar solutions. But, as they found their attitudes and technical approaches in another, they were no doubt encouraged. Coming first were the much-published Miss Mansfield and James Joyce. The tale of the nine years it took before timid publishers and recalcitrant printers would issue *Dubliners* is twice-told. The edition of 1914 published by Grant Richards scarcely sold five hundred copies in its first year.[21] In December, 1916, the work appeared in the United States, and H. L. Mencken, urged by its publisher, B. W. Huebsch, had published two of the stories in *Smart Set*.[22] The Modern Library edition of 1926 made the stories more widely available. The kinship between Joyce's "epiphany" concept of the short story and the focus of Chekhov and Miss Mansfield on moments of revelation has been described by Miss Berkman, who suggests a plausible chain of influences—Turgenev, Chekhov, Mansfield and Turgenev, George Moore, Joyce —to account for the coincidence.[23] Though he is never included in what has become the customary triumvirate, Sherwood Anderson, whose *Winesburg, Ohio* appeared in 1919, importantly influenced the development of the American short story.

Bearing in mind that influence is partly a matter of who came first and that the short story was apparently under intense social pressures which brought about the changes so well worked out in Miss Mansfield's fiction, it perhaps enriches one's view of the literary stream to look at a few relationships which existed.

Virginia Woolf and Katherine Mansfield were interested in one another's work by 1917. This was the year Miss Mansfield wrote happily, "we have got the same job, Virginia, and it is really very curious and thrilling that we should both . . . be after so very nearly the same thing." [24] In this year, too, the Woolfs arranged to bring out "Prelude" under the imprint of their newly founded Hogarth Press; they did so in 1918. But, if there was friendship, it waned the next year. Then, though Miss Mansfield gave *Kew Gardens* an appreciative review in the June *Athenaeum*, her November review of *Night and Day*, a novel traditional in form, expressed mild admiration in comparing it with the work of Jane Austen, and called Mrs. Woolf "unaware of what has been happening." Privately to Murry she wrote, ". . . it is a lie in the soul," objecting to the lack of social conscience and the failure to reflect the war. The following year she did not want Mrs. Woolf to review *Bliss*, "because," as she explained to Murry, "I don't like her work at all at all at all." [25] Reciprocally Mrs. Woolf had not liked the short story of that name when it first appeared in the *English Review:* ". . . the whole conception is poor, cheap, not the vision . . . of an interesting mind." [26]

Be that as it may, Mrs. Woolf's *Monday and Tuesday* is dismissed by David Daiches as "a series of literary exercises rather than of finished works." [27] Impressionistic sketches, these slight performances of 1919 and 1920 were useful in the development of techniques brought to full power in her following novels. The later short works collected posthumously in *A Haunted House* take the form of the modern short story. Of these, "The New Dress" seems to make deliberate reference to Katherine Mansfield's "The Fly." The Woolf story consists of the interior monologue of Mabel Waring, a transcript of her ordeal at a Dalloway party. Her anguish rises from social insecurity but is focused, for her, on the new dress which she herself has designed but has come to feel is unfashionable. She tries to comfort herself with a feeling that she is like the others, but the fly image she employs turns upon her:

> We are all like flies trying to crawl over the edge of the saucer. Mabel thought, and repeated the phrase as if she were crossing herself, as if she were trying to find some spell to annul this pain, to make this agony endurable. . . . Now she could see flies crawling slowly out of a saucer of milk with their wings stuck together. And she strained and strained . . . to make herself see . . . all the other people there as flies, trying to hoist themselves out of something, or into something, meagre, insignificant, toiling flies. But she could not see them like that, not other people. She saw herself like that—she was a fly, but the others were dragonflies, butterflies, beautiful insects . . . while she alone dragged herself up out of the saucer. [28]

Throughout the party her mind dwells on the fly, her unifying image. Her final remark, as she leaves the affair, "Right in the saucer," expresses her feeling of self-derision. Near the end of the story there seems to be an explicit acknowledgement of the Mansfield source: "That wretched fly—where had she read the story that kept coming into her mind about the fly and the saucer? —struggled out."

Similarity in the use of time divisions of a single day, the frames of "At the Bay" and *Mrs. Dalloway*, has been pointed out by Miss Berkman.[29] Again, the use of the sea as the unifying tonal image of that short story is surely related to the elaboration of the same device in *The Waves*. They begin at the same time of day and with very nearly the same sentence:

> MANSFIELD: Very early morning. The sun was not yet risen.
> WOOLF: The sun had not yet risen.[30]

They conceive of the sea as "sleepy" and "a sleeper." Miss Mansfield's opening section introduces a herd of sheep, as light begins to appear. With the rising of her sun, Mrs. Woolf compares the waves to "turbaned warriors . . . who . . . advance upon the feeding flocks, the white sheep" (54). Miss Mansfield's fantasy of the sea's having covered the earth and its houses during the night is echoed in *The Waves*: "Tables and chairs rose to the surface as if they had been sunk under water . . ." (79). The notion is repeated to describe the end of the day: "As if there were waves of darkness in the air, darkness moved on, covering houses, hills, trees, as waves of water wash around the sides of some sunken ship" (168). Their noon sequences describe a burning, pitiless, revealing sun. Of course, both are dealing with the same subject matter, though to different ends; both cultivated highly developed sensibilities as a means to expression. Still, the impressions of "At the Bay" must have left some record, at least, in Mrs. Woolf's subconscious mind, to bear fruit in her later novels.

The important point is not that Virginia Woolf repeats specific images and structural devices used by Katherine Mansfield. The two women display a kinship in craft as they think about how to treat their materials: the extent of the narrator's knowledge, as well as what he will make available to and what he will require of the reader; the increase of dramatic quality in the use

of particular details; the avoidance of narrative passages; the increase of immediacy in the use of interior monologue, and the
freedoms that device allows in dealing with time. Each reflects
the uncertainties of her age: neither will, neither feels that she
should, reach more than implicit conclusions in her writing.
Like Henry James, they "make the reader," requiring that he
grasp their inferences and attain for himself, under their direction, the revelations to which their stories lead. In this kinship of
craftsmanship—no matter how motive, style, or attitude toward
the subject may differ—lies their likeness to James Joyce, to the
writers of the 1920's, and to many followers in modern fiction.

Because, in the 1920's and after, many writers, exploring the
short-story medium with similar needs for expression, moved in
kindred lines of development, it is easy to find a likeness to
Katherine Mansfield in many instances. The more subjective
women writers, such cultivators of sensibility as Elizabeth Bowen
and Eudora Welty, are immediate candidates. Awareness of the
genealogy appears in Ruth M. Vande Kieft's recent study of
Miss Welty:

> Since the central meaning is to be conveyed by indirection, all of these
> writers [Chekhov and Mansfield] have developed their own methods
> of shaping their material with minute care. They invest with maximum
> significance each detail, each small piece of dialogue, narration, or de-
> scription; and they endow each metaphor with an emotional resonance
> comparable to that of poetic metaphor. This care and subtlety in formal
> construction, this lyrical and poetic richness and psychological com-
> plexity, ask for corresponding sympathetic qualities in the reader, as
> does the fiction of James Joyce, Virginia Woolf, and Katherine Anne
> Porter. All of these writers have prepared the way for Miss Welty's
> writing and also for our reading with pleasure and discernment her
> particular kind of fiction.[31]

Miss Bowen's family membership is laid to the *Zeitgeist* by
Sean O'Faolain: ". . . the prime technical characteristic of her
work, as of other modern women writers, such as Virginia Woolf,
is that she fills the vacuum which the general disintegration of
belief has created in life by the pursuit of sensibility." [32] She herself had early noted the resemblance of her work to Miss
Mansfield's.

But here we are pulled up short with a warning proper to all historians too near-sightedly intent on tracing causes and relationships. Miss Bowen has written: "I read *Bliss* when I had completed the first set of my stories which were to make *Encounters*—then admiration and envy were shot through by a profound dismay: I thought: If I ever am published, everybody will say I imitated her. I was right: this happened." [33]

Whatever her influence, Katherine Mansfield stands finally on the longevity of her work. In it there was immaturity, as there must be for those who begin in youth and never reach old age. There were potboilers, as there must be for those who need the money the pen can earn. [34] But even the early, heavily satirical stories of *In a German Pension* can still evoke laughter, to say nothing of recognition from anyone who has boarded for a few weeks with strangers. The observation from the first was of reality, which the overreaching of youthful antagonisms cannot dispel. Miss Mansfield could see, and she taught her reader to see.

And to hear. Talk is a large part of the subject in the first stories —the interminable, banal chatter of the German pensioners, who steadily expose their ignorance, greed, chauvinism, and selfishness. Even with the excessive comments of an undisciplined narrator, the talk reveals more of Miss Mansfield's disdain than she overtly states. Already a deft selection of materials is her means of communication; indirection is her chosen method. She had an ear for distinctions among speakers, and she did not lose it. There is a terseness in the language of nobility not matched by the German bourgeoisie, whether romantic or practical. A structural nuance in the dialogue reminds the reader, too, that this is not the speech of the English.

In fact, the notion that Miss Mansfield's style is all too frequently the same for all her characters, a style that reflects her own feminine voice—"fluttery, gossipy, breathless" [35]— disregards a large portion of her work and misreads her intention. The early naturalistic New Zealand characterizations explored the possibilities of dialect with acumen. The speech of the ignorant is not forgotten in the monologues of the lady's maid and Ma Parker or the conversation of Mrs. Stubbs and Alice in "At the Bay." Mansfield children always speak with their strange, concrete directness. The emasculated speech patterns and diction of Raoul Duquette and lesser members of his band, such as Eddie Warren and Bobbie Kane, are unmistakable. More substantial is the tone of Stanley Burnell and his counterpart John Hammond, yet it is quite different from the understated worldliness of the men of "The Escape" and "The Man without a Temperament."

Miss Mansfield dissects many fluttery women, but the voice of Moira Morrison or Isabel of "Marriage à la Mode" is not her voice, nor, unless in memory of her adolescence, do the many young girls speak for her. The vague disconnection of the colonel's daughters is unlike any of the rest. If there is any alliance between the thought processes and speech of her characters and Katherine Mansfield, it probably is reflected in such wary protagonists as Vera in "A Dill Pickle" and the unnamed woman of "Psychology." In her mature work Miss Mansfield herself does not appear. The voice she selects is chosen for its meaning within the story.

Her characters are memorable for the moments of discovery in which they speak, aloud or to themselves. Usually the emphasis is on a larger concept than the description of an individual. "I seen the little lamp" concentrates for the reader any number of affirmative stands. In Bertha Young's final observations—" 'Oh, what is going to happen now?' . . . But the pear tree was as lovely as ever and as full of flower and as still"—the wonder and terror of life are juxtaposed. A larger will to isolation than John Hammond's is exposed when he tells himself that "They would never be alone together again."

As Elizabeth Bowen has pointed out, the short story is not the medium for full character development, and Miss Mansfield did well in perceiving this limit of the form.[36] Thus, if her characters are to take on depth, it is usually in the New Zealand stories, where the same people are met again and again. The reader's intimacy with Stanley Burnell, Kezia, Beryl, and even the aloof Linda increases until it is as if Miss Mansfield had written the novel she hoped for when she began work on "Prelude." [37] Her depth is evident in the sympathy extended to all these individuals, so very much at cross-purposes.

Stories of diverse scenes also overlay one another, the awareness of one increasing the understanding of another. As with most writers, certain themes, subjects, and images preoccupy Katherine

Mansfield. Her study of isolated women ranges from the nervi-
ness of Monica Tyrell through the valiant sensitivities of Miss
Brill to the rebellious desire for "life" of Beryl and the secretive
independence of Kezia. At a tangent to this subject are the variety
of married women who are also alone: the hysterical, compen-
sating Bertha Young; the shallow Isabel torn between the values
of Bohemia and her husband; the withdrawn Linda Burnell;
Janey Hammond, the stranger; and the uneasily dependent invalid of "The Man without a Temperament."

Of overbearing businessmen fathers, one of her so-called obsessive subjects,[38] it is a long distance from "Bottlenose" in her
Scrapbook[39] to the harried disciplinarian of "Sixpence." Relationships of such men with their families are not always those of the
irascible colonel; they may reflect the puzzled fatigue of old Mr.
Neave. The ego of Stanley Burnell is very different from, much
more humane than, the ego of Reginald Peacock. Different again
is that of John Hammond, the self-made stranger. While the boss,
unlike but as abstract and ominous as the figures of the early
"Child-Who-Was-Tired," is intricately as much symbol as man,
though the man is still wretchedly, frighteningly human.

There is, perhaps, a greater sameness in the excited, half-
formed, adolescent young women who reach out impatiently
for a romantic image of "life," but Laura after the garden party
can rise to an incoherent insight. And the young men, as they
grow a little older, can look back upon themselves with jaded
sophistication. The passionate innocent of "Something Childish But Very Natural" may be on the way to his "poison" in "Mr.
and Mrs. Dove." The protagonist of "The Escape" has avoided
the life-denying losses of "The Man without a Temperament."

Considering all this variety—and there is more—it is odd to
read of the limitations which Miss Mansfield's experience imposed on her subject matter. Every writer is so limited. What did
Tolstoi know beyond the Caucasian wars, his serfs, the society
he moved in, and a little history? Has not William Faulkner
mined the provincial Mississippi county that was apparently
his most informing experience? It is not scope that matters to
literature but depth. Clarence Buddington Kelland has probably
exploited a hundred widespread scenes with the same combina-
tions of "characters," the same stereotyped plot; yet some readers

will not recognize his name. Katherine Mansfield wrote of a small part of New Zealand, of London literary life, of children, servants, and boardinghouse inmates. But the limit to her treatment of what she saw was only the limit of time: she died before she could write all her stories. Perhaps because her social and geographical range was small, her penetration was intensified.

She did not need many different scenes, for she used setting, like character, only to convey meaning. If she chose to describe a place, her work was vivid, specific in detail, but impressionistic. The labored blueprints of an Arnold Bennett were not necessary to the sense of location. A little data would give the tone of the experience to unfold there or characterize the person to whom the scene was meaningful. The significant items in John Hammond's hotel room are the bed and the dying fire, and they are enough to image his emotional disaster. Though the doll's house is described in great detail, illumination at last focuses around the little lamp. As the boss in "The Fly" points to his new office furniture, the reader sees, as well, the man and the quality of his avowed grief. Geographical juxtaposition of rich and poor in "The Garden-Party" emblems the simultaneity of frivolity and death; the sea, in many aspects, dominates the activities and meaning of "At the Bay." Miss Mansfield kept under sharp control her capacity for poetic description, subordinating such passages always to her larger purpose. Even in stories which fail because of inadequate conception, her concern for form prevents lack of control.

This formal care, the restriction of meaning to the implicit, the awareness of paradox and the resulting avoidance of dogma —in all these characteristics Katherine Mansfield is in the mainstream (and in advance of it) of modern fiction. In her variety of treatment, depth of perception, and formal precision, but most of all in the continuing aliveness and immediate relevance of her stories, rests her claim to a place in literary history.

At such a position, however, she might have smiled. It was communication that mattered to this woman, who wrote so often of the inadequacy of human contacts. Sometimes she cared only for the appraisal of her friends: Murry, Walter De la Mare, George Santayana, a few others. Once, wondering about the public reception of a story, she wrote Murry, "Tell me if anybody says they like it, will you? . . . It's just a queer feeling—after one has dropped a pebble in. Will there be a ripple or not?" [40] One recorded moment of triumph came when she heard that the printer who set the type for "Prelude" had said of her manuscript, "My! but these kids are real!" [41] This was the reward, the goal achieved. She had told the truth, and someone had seen it. It was enough.

Notes and References

Chapter One

1. Rachel Allbright in "Katherine Mansfield and Wingley," *Folio*, XXIV, iii (1959), 23-29, has written of the cats in Miss Mansfield's life.

2. *Katherine Mansfield's Letters to John Middleton Murry, 1913-1922*, ed. John Middleton Murry (New York, 1951), p. 516. Hereafter this volume will be referred to as *Letters*.

3. "The Apple-Tree," in *The Scrapbook of Katherine Mansfield*, ed. J. Middleton Murry (New York, 1940), p. 28; and in *Journal of Katherine Mansfield*, ed. J. Middleton Murry (London, 1954), p. 87. Hereafter these volumes will be referred to as *Scrapbook* and *Journal*.

4. For Miss Mansfield's life I rely largely on the excellent biography by Antony Alpers, *Katherine Mansfield: A Biography* (New York, 1954). Further details are found in Sylvia Berkman, *Katherine Mansfield: A Critical Study* (New Haven, 1951), which provides the most reliable bibliographical data.

5. Alpers, p. 50.

6. *Journal*, p. 103.

7. *Journal*, pp. 2-4.

8. There can be little doubt that Miss Mansfield read the translations in Anton Tschechoff, *Die Bauern*, Einzig autorisierte Ausgabe aus dem Russischen übersetzt von Wladimir Czumikow (Gesammelte Werke, Band IV), Verlegt bei Eugen Diederichs in Leipzig, 1902.

9. *Journal*, p. 58.

10. *Ibid.*

11. *Ibid.*, p. 90.

12. She wrote letters of enthusiastic excitement to Murry while composing this story. See *Letters*, pp. 149, 151, 158, 160-61, 163, and see above, Chapter 4.

13. *A Writer's Diary*, ed. Leonard Woolf (New York, 1954), p. 12.

14. Ronald Sutherland in "Katherine Mansfield: Plagiarist, Disciple, or Ardent Admirer?" *Critique*, V (1962), 58-76, accepts this view of

Alpers and Berkman and argues further that Miss Mansfield did not ever learn her craft from Chekhov.

15. Richard Ellman, *James Joyce* (New York, 1959), pp. 218, 364. Lack of comment in Miss Mansfield's writing suggests that she was unfamiliar with the short stories, but she did know *Ulysses* and *Portrait of the Artist as a Young Man.*

16. *The Letters of Katherine Mansfield,* ed. J. Middleton Murry (New York, 1929), I, 71. Since this publication appeared in two volumes, it will also be referred to hereafter as *Letters.*

17. Austin McGiffert Wright, in *The American Short Story in the Twenties* (Chicago, 1961), has painstakingly analyzed the differences in subject matter, form, and technique between the American short story of the 1920's and earlier American stories. No similar account of British fiction has appeared; however, perhaps because the dominant influences are the same on both sides of the Atlantic, his conclusions are useful in distinguishing the modern from the traditional short story in England.

Chapter Two

1. Elisabeth Schneider in "Katherine Mansfield and Chekhov," *Modern Language Notes,* L (1935), 396, attributes the close parallels to "unconscious memory." Alpers, *Katherine Mansfield,* pp. 130-32, regards the likeness as "indisputable plagiarism," although he thinks that Miss Mansfield had developed the same method in "The Tiredness of Rosabel" before she read Chekhov. Miss Berkman, in *Katherine Mansfield,* feels that the adaptation was probably conscious.

2. Sutherland, "Katherine Mansfield: Plagiarist, Disciple, or Ardent Admirer?" p. 70.

3. *Ibid.,* pp. 72, 75. Mr. Sutherland overlooks (p. 63) Chekhov's influence on *In a German Pension.*

4. Anton Tschechoff, *Ein bekannter Herr: Humoristische Geschichte,* trans. Wladimir Czumikow (Jena, 1910).

5. Pogglioli, *The Phoenix and the Spider* (Cambridge, Mass., 1957), p. 110.

6. During this period two other stories were printed: "Mary," in the *Idler,* March, 1910, and "A Fairy Story," in the *Open Window,* December, 1910. See Berkman, p. 213, n. 10, for data on poems of this period.

7. Paul Selver, *Orage and the New Age Circle* (London, 1959), pp. 17, 26, 46.

8. *Letters,* p. 467. As the surrounding letters of that spring reveal, Miss Mansfield was hard pressed for money, so much so that by April, one day after violently rejecting excisions from "Je ne Parle pas Fran-

çais"—"shall I pick the eyes out of a story for £ 40?"—she felt compelled to reconsider, as usual trusting Murry's judgment: "If you agree to what they say—why then, all's well (and I DO want the money)." (*Letters*, p. 515.) He had even persuaded her in February (*Letters*, p. 477) to reissue *In a German Pension*, but this did not occur in her lifetime.

9. Alpers, p. 303.

10. Murry's dating is not always reliable. The touring journal manner and the fact that Miss Mansfield did travel briefly to Bruges and Geneva in July, 1911, suggest a later date for the two stories.

11. Major differences between Miss Mansfield's story and Chekhov's are these children, the elimination of an apprentice who has no function in the earlier work and of realistic flashbacks concerning the child's life, and the shift from a realistic, muddy road to an unreal, white road in her vision. The perceptions of the story are entirely Miss Mansfield's.

12. Bashkirtseff, *The Journal of a Young Artist: 1860-1884*, trans. Mary J. Serrano (New York, 1889), p. 142: "*Sic transit gloriā Ducis.*" Anti-German feeling is also evident, as on pp. 138-39.

13. For Frau Brechenmacher's sensitive response to the music, Miss Mansfield borrowed the last clause of "The Tiredness of Rosabel": "she smiled with a little nervous tremor around the mouth."

14. Miss Mansfield was in Bavaria between June, 1909, and January, 1910.

15. *Journal of Katherine Mansfield*, ed. J. Middleton Murry (London, 1954), p. 42.

16. Her later evaluation of this sort of "cleverness" is evident in "Je ne Parle pas Français," when Duquette congratulates himself on such phrase-framing.

17. This remark probably reflects not only Miss Mansfield's response to her miscarriage in Bavaria but also the influence of Beatrice Hastings, an assistant editor of the *New Age*, who, according to Philip Mairet in *A. R. Orage: A Memoir* (London, 1936), p. 51, had written an article pleading that the state protect women from the "horrors of giving birth." Sometime before May, 1911, Miss Hastings assisted Miss Mansfield in obtaining an abortion (Alpers, p. 140). Murry in *Journal*, p. 44, doubts that there was an abortion.

18. "The Breidenbach Family in England" was unsigned and apparently Murry remained unaware of it. The ascription is due to Miss Berkman, p. 212, n. 6. Also in the *New Age* at this time appeared the uncollected "Festival of the Coronation."

19. The whole scene is clearly New Zealand, not Germany at all. See Berkman, p. 216, n. 26.

20. See *Letters*, p. 148: "I simply loathe and abominate the French bourgeoisie."

21. Alpers, pp. 144-45.

Chapter Three

1. Murry, *Between Two Worlds: An Autobiography* (London, 1935), p. 184.

2. *Ibid.*, p. 216.

3. Alpers, *Katherine Mansfield*, pp. 187, 194.

4. These are the German names which appeared in *Rhythm;* they were changed in Murry's posthumous collection of the stories to *Helen* and *Dr. Malcolm.* The Binzer family, clearly that of "A Birthday," became *Carstairs.* Murry dates the story 1910.

5. The fears and nightmares are Murry's, as he recalled them in *Between Two Worlds* (pp. 16, 24), but apparently he only *saw* children beaten when he peeped through a fence at his boisterous neighbors or observed canings at school (*ibid.*, pp. 21, 39).

6. *The Scrapbook of Katherine Mansfield*, ed. J. Middleton Murry (New York, 1940), p. 14.

7. *Rhythm*, II (June, 1912), 35. She is kinder to Strindberg, who attracts and repels her; hilarious in a skit, written with Murry, on a play by J. M. Synge.

8. *Rhythm*, II (June, 1912) and (July, 1912), 37-39.

9. The story is dedicated to Anne Estelle Rice, a *Fauve* whose work often appeared in *Rhythm*.

10. *New Age*, March 28, 1912.

11. *New Age*, February 6, 1913.

12. *New Age*, May 15, 1913.

13. *Letters*, pp. 5-7.

14. *Scrapbook*, p. 50.

15. Murry, *Between Two Worlds*, p. 324.

16. *Ibid.*, pp. 348-50, 353, 357.

17. Alpers, p. 208, quotes Lawrence in a letter to Cynthia Asquith.

18. *Scrapbook*, pp. 28-31; *Journal*, p. 89.

Chapter Four

1. *The Short Stories of Katherine Mansfield*, intro. J. Middleton Murry (New York, 1950), p. vii.

2. *Journal of Katherine Mansfield*, pp. 93-94.

3. Berkman, *Katherine Mansfield*, p. 71: "The form and nature of her earlier stories she rejected: 'No novels, no problem stories, nothing that is not simple, open.'"

4. *Journal*, p. 93.

5. *Letters,* p. 166.

6. The first-person narrator of the 1915 version of "The Wind Blows" was changed to third-person for 1921 publication in *Bliss and Other Stories.*

7. Erich Auerbach, *Mimesis,* trans. Williard R. Trask (Garden City, New York, 1957), pp. 471-74.

8. *Letters,* p. 380. Here she complained that the war was ignored in Virginia Woolf's *Night and Day:* ". . . it is a lie in the soul. . . . the novel just can't leave the war out. . . . I feel in the *profoundest* sense that nothing can ever be the same—that, as artists, we are traitors if we feel otherwise; we have to take it into account and find new expressions, new moulds for our new thoughts and feelings."

9. *Letters,* p. 149. Murry explains in a note that the French phrase refers to a Provençal poem by Henri Fabre, "telling of the withering of the almond blossom by the cold."

10. Katherine Mansfield, *The Aloe* (London, 1930), p. 85.

11. Kezia's fear, as imaged in *The Aloe,* pp. 17-18, is very much like Linda's.

12. *The Aloe,* p. 139: "And she dreamed that she and her mother were caught up on the cold water and into the ship. . . . She saw her mother sitting quietly in the boat, sunning herself in the moonlight, as she expressed it. No, after all, it would be better if her mother did not come. . . ."

13. *Letters,* I, 74.

14. *Journal,* pp. 109-12; *Scrapbook,* pp. 58-60.

15. Murry, *Between Two Worlds,* p. 464.

16. *Letters,* p. 151.

17. This ending is richer in implication than that of the earlier version, handset by Murry and his brother Richard. Their Heron Press edition reads, on page 91, after "No, not yet, Madame": "I'd rather like to dine with her. Even to sleep with her afterwards. Would she be pale like that all over? But no. She'd have large moles. They go with that kind of skin. And I can't bear them. They remind me somehow, disgustingly, of mushrooms." This passage and others are cited in M. Distel's "Katherine Mansfield's Erzählung *Je ne parle pas français:* Ein Beitrag zur Interpretation anhand der Originalfassung," *Neueren Sprachen,* No. 2 (1959), pp. 249-63, as evidence that Murry, in the revisions for *Bliss and Other Stories,* distorted the story. It is hard to reconcile this theory with the fact that the original printing was entirely due to Murry's efforts.

18. *Letters,* p. 259.

19. *Ibid.,* p. 393.

Chapter Five

1. *Letters*, p. 161.
2. *Ibid.*, p. 180.
3. *Ibid.*, p. 546.
4. *Ibid.*, p. 170.
5. *Scrapbook*, pp. 34-44.
6. I am indebted to Professor Jan Lawson Hinely of the University of Illinois for the germ of this idea.
7. Murry, *Katherine Mansfield and Other Literary Portraits* (London, [1949]), p. 9.
8. Berkman, *Katherine Mansfield*, pp. 180, 183.
9. *Letters*, p. 211.
10. I am indebted to my colleague, Professor Marie N. Ohlsen of California State College at Los Angeles, for this suggestion. It might be added that the beginning of *Pearl* is *pear*, and in French and German the pronunciation of the name is similar to that of *peril* in English. Word-play on names is frequent in Miss Mansfield's work, though rarely this subtle.
11. *Letters*, p. 577.
12. Berkman, p. 107.
13. *Letters*, p. 604.
14. *Ibid.*, pp. 604-5.
15. That the story also expresses a crucial disillusionment with Murry is evident from the December, 1920, entries in the *Scrapbook*, pp. 88-89, expanded in the *Journal*, pp. 227-30.
16. Cf. the sensitive explication of Donald W. Kleine, "Katherine Mansfield and the Prisoner of Love," *Critique*, III (1960), 20-33. Kleine notes the word-play on *Salesby* but interprets it differently.
17. The phrase comes from the penetrating analysis of structure, irony, and symbolism in Peter Thorpe's "Teaching 'Miss Brill,'" *College English*, XXIII (1962), 661-63.
18. *Letters*, p. 598.
19. *Ibid.*, p. 594.
20. *Journal*, p. 263.
21. *Journal*, pp. 228-29.
22. A suggestive analysis of the time aspect of the story appears in Wallace Stegner, Richard Scowcraft, and Boris Ilyin, *The Writer's Art: A Collection of Short Stories* (Boston, 1950), pp. 74-77.
23. *Letters*, II, 454.

Notes and References

Chapter Six

1. *Letters,* pp. 583-84.
2. Alpers, *Katherine Mansfield,* p. 309, discovered from the original manuscript that Josephine is forty-three; Constantia, thirty-eight.
3. *Letters,* II, 389.
4. *Ibid.,* p. 210.
5. *Ibid.,* pp. 116, 423. Other references to flies are noted by Celeste T. Wright in "Genesis of a Short Story," *Philological Quarterly,* XXXIV (1955), 91-96, and by Berkman, *Katherine Mansfield,* pp. 193-94.
6. Berkman, p. 194.
7. Celeste T. Wright, as above, and in *Explicator,* XII (1954), 27; Willis D. Jacobs, *Explicator,* V (1947), 32.
8. J. D. Thomas in "Symbol and Parallelism in 'The Fly,'" *College English,* XXII (1962), 261, points this out, but stresses their contrast, which is also evident. Notes 9-14 indicate similarities between my interpretation and those of other explicators. Ultimately, I agree with none of these.
9. Cf. R. A. Jolly's reply to Bateson (n. 12 below) in *Essays in Criticism,* XII (1962), 338.
10. This play on the word *life,* Stanley B. Greenfield in *Explicator,* XVII (1958), 2, says, is Miss Mansfield's "supreme achievement in this story. Time and life are too much for any man; . . . the past and its grief must yield. . . ."
11. Cf. R. A. Copland's reply to Bateson (n. 12 below) in *Essays in Criticism,* XII (1962), 340.
12. Robert W. Stallman in *Explicator,* III (1945), 49, is, I believe, the first critic to note that to the boss all three men are like flies and that the boss is himself alternately identified and not identified with the fly. Jolly, pp. 336-37, sees Woodifield, Macey, and perhaps the boss as flies. F. W. Bateson and B. Shahevitch in "Katherine Mansfield's 'The Fly': A Critical Exercise," *Essays in Criticism,* XII (1962), 51, sees a dual element of "sadistic tenderness" in the boss's relations with his son and Woodifield.
13. Cf. Bateson, p. 51.
14. I believe this analysis clarifies the meaning of the dualism suggested by Stallman, *Explicator,* III (1945), 49, and resolves the inconsistency found in this dualism by Berkman, p. 195. Cf. E. B. Greenwood's reply to Bateson in *Essays in Criticism,* XII (1962), 346-47.
15. "Last Talks with Katherine Mansfield," *Century Magazine,* N.S., LXXXVII (1924), 36-40; Murry in *Letters,* pp. 699-701.
16. *The Novel and the Modern World* (Chicago, 1939), Chapters 1 and 5. Austin M. Wright in *The American Short Story in the Twen-*

ties, p. 273, quotes a similar explanation of Joyce's experimentation, taken from Harry Levin's *James Joyce: A Critical Introduction* (Norfolk, Conn., 1941), p. 28. Cf. Wright, p. 150.

17. Wright, pp. 266-67.

18. *Ibid.*, pp. 272, 150.

19. *Mimesis,* pp. 482-83, 487-88.

20. Berkman, p. 2.

21. Richard Ellman, *James Joyce* (New York, 1959), p. 364, note, states that 379 copies were sold by May 1, 1915, "including the 120 bought by Joyce." On p. 412 Ellman states that 499 copies were sold in 1914; 26 in the first six months of 1915; and 7 in the last half of that year. The discrepancy in the figures appears to be the result of adding Joyce's 120 to the original 379 and ignoring the 26.

22. *Ibid.*, p. 395.

23. Berkman, pp. 159-60.

24. *Letters,* I, 71.

25. *Letters,* pp. 380, 606.

26. Woolf, *A Writer's Diary,* p. 2.

27. *Virginia Woolf* (Norfolk, Conn., 1942), pp. 43-52.

28. Virginia Woolf, *A Haunted House* (London, 1953), pp. 50-51.

29. Berkman, pp. 168-69.

30. *The Waves* (London, 1953), p. 5. Page references in the text hereafter are to this volume.

31. *Eudora Welty* (New York, 1962), pp. 180-81.

32. *The Vanishing Hero* (Boston, 1957), p. 167.

33. *Early Stories* (New York, 1951), p. viii.

34. Miss Mansfield's allowance from her father was never adequate, nor, it seems, could Murry sufficiently supplement her income to pay for the expenses caused by her continuing bout with tuberculosis. Cf. Alpers, pp. 361-66.

35. Cf. H. E. Bates, *The Modern Short Story* (London, 1941), p. 129, and the criticism of his remarks in Berkman, pp. 177-84. I am not in complete agreement with her view of "Bliss" and of "Marriage à la Mode."

36. Katherine Mansfield, *Stories,* intro. Elizabeth Bowen (New York, 1960), p. xxi.

37. Cf. Berkman, pp. 199-202.

38. See the psychological studies of Celeste T. Wright, as listed in the bibliography.

39. *Scrapbook,* p. 50.

40. *Letters,* p. 628.

41. *The Short Stories of Katherine Mansfield,* p. vii.

Selected Bibliography

WORKS OF KATHERINE MANSFIELD

I. Fiction (*Stories collected in each volume are listed in chronological order of publication. Only first editions are given.*)

In a German Pension. London: Stephen Swift, 1911.
(All stories previously published appeared in the *New Age*, as dated.)
"The Child-Who-Was-Tired," February 24, 1910.
"Germans at Meat," March 3, 1910.
"The Baron," March 10, 1910.
"The Luft Bad," March 24, 1910.
"At Lehmann's," July 7, 1910.
"Frau Brechenmacher Attends a Wedding," July 21, 1910.
"The Sister of the Baroness," August 4, 1910.
"Frau Fischer," August 18, 1910.
"A Birthday," May 18, 1911.
"The Modern Soul," June 22, 1911.
"The Advanced Lady" (not previously published).
"The Swing of the Pendulum" (not previously published).
"A Blaze" (not previously published).

Prelude. Richmond: Hogarth Press, 1918.
Je ne Parle pas Français. Hampstead: Heron Press, 1920.
Bliss and Other Stories. London: Constable, 1920.
"The Wind Blows," *Signature,* October 18, 1915 (as "Autumn II").
"The Little Governess," *Signature,* October 18 and November 1, 1915.
"Mr. Reginald Peacock's Day," *New Age,* June 14, 1917.
"Feuille d'Album," *New Age,* September 20, 1917 (as "An Album Leaf").
"A Dill Pickle," *New Age,* October 4, 1917.

"Prelude," as above.

"Bliss," *English Review*, August, 1918.

"Pictures," *Arts and Letters*, Autumn, 1919.

"Je ne Parle pas Français," as above.

"The Man without a Temperament," *Arts and Letters*, Spring, 1920.

"Revelations," *Athenaeum*, June 11, 1920.

"The Escape," *Athenaeum*, July 9, 1920.

"Sun and Moon," *Athenaeum*, October 1, 1920.

"Psychology" (not previously published).

The Garden-Party and Other Stories. London: Constable, 1922.

"Bank Holiday," *Athenaeum*, August 6, 1920.

"The Young Girl," *Athenaeum*, August 29, 1920.

"Miss Brill," *Athenaeum*, November 26, 1920.

"The Lady's Maid," *Athenaeum*, December 24, 1920.

"The Stranger," *London Mercury*, January, 1921.

"The Life of Ma Parker," *Nation*, February 26, 1921.

"The Daughters of the Late Colonel," *London Mercury*, May, 1921.

"Mr. and Mrs. Dove," *Sphere*, August 13, 1921.

"An Ideal Family," *Sphere*, August 20, 1921.

"Her First Ball," *Sphere*, November 28, 1921.

"The Voyage," *Sphere*, December 24, 1921.

"Marriage à la Mode," *Sphere*, December 31, 1921.

"At the Bay," *London Mercury*, January, 1922.

"The Garden-Party," *Weekly Westminster Gazette*, February 4, 11, 18, 1922.

"The Singing Lesson" (not previously published).

The Dove's Nest and Other Stories. London: Constable, 1923.

"The Doll's House," *Nation*, February 4, 1922.

"Taking the Veil," *Sketch*, February 22, 1922.

"The Fly," *Nation*, March 18, 1922.

"Honeymoon," *Nation*, April 29, 1922.

"A Cup of Tea," *Story-Teller*, May, 1922.

"The Canary," *Nation*, April 21, 1923.

(Other stories in this volume were unfinished at Miss Mansfield's death and, consequently, were not previously published.)

Something Childish and Other Stories. London: Constable, 1924. (Also under title *The Little Girl and Other Stories*. New York: Knopf, 1924.)

Selected Bibliography

"The Journey to Bruges," *New Age*, August 24, 1911.
"A Truthful Adventure," *New Age*, September 7, 1911.
"The Woman at the Store," *Rhythm*, Spring, 1912.
"How Pearl Button Was Kidnapped," *Rhythm*, September, 1912
"The Little Girl," *Rhythm*, October, 1912.
"New Dresses," *Rhythm*, October, 1912.
"Ole Underwood," *Rhythm*, January, 1913.
"Pension Séguin," *Blue Review*, May, 1913.
"Millie," *Blue Review*, June, 1913.
"Violet," *Blue Review*, June, 1913.
"Bains Turcs," *Blue Review*, July, 1913.
"Two Tuppenny Ones, Please," *New Age*, May 3, 1917.
"Late at Night," *New Age*, May 10, 1917.
"The Black Cap," *New Age*, May 17, 1917.
"Sixpence," *Sphere*, August 6, 1921.
"Poison," *Collier's*, November 24, 1923.
"A Suburban Fairy Tale," *Adelphi*, December, 1923.
"Something Childish But Very Natural," *Collier's*, January 5, 1924.
"The Tiredness of Rosabel," *Collier's*, February 9, 1924.
"See-Saw," *Adelphi*, July, 1924.
(The following were not previously published.)
    "Carnation."
    "An Indiscreet Journey."
    "Spring Pictures."
    "This Flower."
    "Wrong House."

The Aloe. London: Constable, 1930.

II. Other Writing (Dates and publishers are those of editions to which I have had access.)

Journal of Katherine Mansfield, ed. J. Middleton Murry. London: Constable, 1954.
The Letters of Katherine Mansfield, ed. J. Middleton Murry. New York Knopf, 1929.
Reminiscences of Leonid Andreyev, by Maxim Gorki, trans. Katherine Mansfield and S. S. Koteliansky. London: Hogarth Press, 1948.
Novels and Novelists, ed. J. Middleton Murry. London: Constable, 1930.
Poems. London: Constable, 1923.
The Scrapbook of Katherine Mansfield, ed. J. Middleton Murry. New York: Knopf, 1940.

Katherine Mansfield's Letters to John Middleton Murry, 1913-1922,
ed. John Middleton Murry. New York: Knopf, 1951.

WORKS RELATED TO KATHERINE MANSFIELD

I. Studies (*Explications of single stories are not included.*)

ALPERS, ANTONY. *Katherine Mansfield: A Biography.* New York: Knopf,
1954. The definitive biography.
BERKMAN, SYLVIA. *Katherine Mansfield: A Critical Study.* New Haven:
Yale University Press, 1951. An excellent study of the relationships
of Mansfield's life and work; valuable corrections of Mantz bibliography.
COX, SYDNEY. "The Fastidiousness of Katherine Mansfield," *Sewanee
Review,* XXXIX (1931), 158-69. Indicates how the Mansfield
focus on specific detail involves the reader in the fictional experience; summarizes her objectives, her challenge to evil in life.
HUBBELL, GEORGE SHELTON. "Katherine Mansfield and Kezia," *Sewanee
Review,* XXXV (1927), 325-35. A sensitive appreciation of Mansfield's respect for childhood, suggesting adult meanings in Kezia's
responses.
HYNES, SAM. "Katherine Mansfield: The Defeat of the Personal," *South
Atlantic Quarterly,* LII (1953), 555-60. A negative appraisal,
which finds the moral structure of Mansfield's work inadequate,
immature in its failure to compromise with reality.
MANTZ, RUTH ELVISH. *The Critical Bibliography of Katherine Mansfield.* London: Constable, 1931. Nearly complete, subject to cor-
rection by Berkman; compiled with Murry's cooperation and
contains information from him on publication history of some
works.
MURRY, JOHN MIDDLETON. *Between Two Worlds: An Autobiography.*
London: Jonathan Cape, 1935. At Chapter XIV takes up his life
with Katherine Mansfield from 1912 through 1918.
MURRY, JOHN MIDDLETON. *Katherine Mansfield and Other Literary
Studies.* London: Constable, 1959. Chapter II gives a sympathetic
but biased account of Mansfield's achievement, the finding of
serenity after conflicting perceptions of good and evil.
WAGENKNECHT, EDWARD. "Katherine Mansfield," *English Journal,*
XVII (1928), 272-84. An appreciation; suggests a relationship of
her humor to that of Charles Dickens.
WRIGHT, CELESTE T. "Darkness as a Symbol in Katherine Mansfield,"
Modern Philology, LI (1954), 204-207. A study of tunnels and
dark waters as obsessive symbols, rising from an actual fear in
childhood of darkness.

Selected Bibliography

————. "Katherine Mansfield and the 'Secret Smile,'" *Literature and Psychology*, V (1955), 44-48. A study of the recurrent "smile" image, reflecting Mansfield's sense that she was an unwanted child.

————. "Katherine Mansfield's Dog Image," *Literature and Psychology*, X (1960), 80-81. A study of the dog image as a symbol of fear or a death phobia.

————. "Katherine Mansfield's Father Image," in *The Image of the Work*, ed. B. H. Lehman *et al.*, University of California Publications: English Studies, 11 (Berkeley and Los Angeles: University of California Press, 1955), pp. 137-55. A psychological study of the effect of a father complex on Mansfield's work.

II. Background

AUERBACH, ERICH. *Mimesis*. Garden City, New York: Doubleday, 1957. Chapter 20 contains a study of the representation of reality in twentieth-century literature.

BASHKIRTSEFF, MARIE. *The Journal of a Young Artist, 1860-1884*, trans. Mary J. Serrano. New York: Cassell, 1889. Mansfield's adolescent reading.

CHEKHOV, ANTON. *The Tales of Chekhov*, trans. Constance Garnett. New York: Macmillan, 1917-1923. 13 vols. A significant influence.

DAICHES, DAVID. *The Novel and the Modern World*. Chicago: University of Chicago Press, 1939. Chapter 5 examines Mansfield's technique, her individualized search for truth as characteristic of contemporary literature.

JOYCE, JAMES. *Dubliners*. New York: Random House (Modern Library), 1926.

MAIRET, PHILIP. *A. R. Orage: A Memoir*. London: Dent, 1936. Describes the *New Age* environment.

POGGLIOLI, RENATA. *The Phoenix and the Spider*. Cambridge, Mass.: Harvard University Press, 1957. Chapter 4 is a useful study of the development of Chekhov's short-story technique.

SELVER, PAUL. *Orage and the New Age Circle*. London: Allen and Unwin, 1959. Describes the *New Age* environment.

WRIGHT, AUSTIN McGIFFERT. *The American Short Story in the Twenties*. Chicago: University of Chicago Press, 1961. A useful analysis.

III. Periodicals

The Adelphi, I (June, 1923-May, 1924); II (June, 1924-May, 1925).
The Athenaeum, April 4, 1919-February 11, 1921.
The Blue Review, I (May-July, 1913).
The New Age, N.S., VI (November, 1909-April, 1910); VII (May-October, 1910); IX (May-October, 1911); X (November, 1911-April, 1912); XVIII (November, 1915-April, 1916); XXI (May-October, 1917).
Rhythm, I-II (Summer, 1911-March, 1913).
The Signature, I (October 4-November 1, 1915).

Index

Index

Index